How to be an Expert Driver

The practical guide to better driving

Jane Gregory BA (Hons), PGCE

D0353405

AA Publishing

Written by: Jane Gregory
Consultants: Jennifer Ellingford, ADI
                Pete Fane, ADI
                Andrew Howard, Head of Road Safety, AA
                Sue Hubbard, ADI, Business Development Manager,
                     AA The Driving School
                Keith Lane, BSc DE, Dip Adv DI, IAM
                Eddy Wilde, ADI
                The author would also like to thank Nick Charles (AA
                Telematics), Dr Mark Horswill (University of Reading), Nick
                Otway, John Stubbs, Trudy Thompson (Womens Motoring
                Service) and Paul Stonehouse for their invaluable assistance.

Copy editor: Pam Stagg
Artwork: Chris Orr & Associates

Published by AA Publishing, a trading name of Automobile Association
Developments Ltd, whose registered office is at Millstream, Maidenhead Road,
Windsor, Berkshire SL4 5GD.

A CIP catalogue record for this book is available from the British Library.

ISBN 0 7495 3156 8 paperback
ISBN 0 7495 3254 8 hardback

Origination by Anton Graphics, Andover
Printed and bound in Spain by Graficas Estella, S.A.

Find out more about the AA on **www.theAA.com**

Contents

Introduction

Improving your driving skills

Think back, for a moment, to the day when you passed your test. Among the feelings of elation and relief was probably the thought, 'I'll never need to have another driving lesson in my life!' But events since that time – perhaps an accident involving you or a friend, or increasing responsibilities for others – may have given you cause to reconsider.

The requirements for the driving test represent just the start of the complex set of skills and mental abilities that make up driving today. Anticipation and forward planning are vital, and drivers have to learn to 'read the road' ahead in order to decide well in advance whether to slow down or maintain speed, overtake or give way, change lanes or stay in a line of traffic – being able to

Up to 65% of all company vehicles are involved in accidents each year.

control the car safely is only the first layer of the demanding activity we undertake every time we set out on the road. Drivers must be constantly alert, never assuming that other road users will behave in a safe or predictable manner.

The speed and volume of traffic on our roads has increased dramatically in recent years, and the demands on drivers have increased significantly too. 'Sunday drivers' are no longer a familiar sight, as few people now would rate 'going for a run in the car' as a relaxing pastime.

Driving, of course, involves much more than carrying out the mechanical processes that cause the vehicle to move in the desired direction. On most journeys (except those of a routine or daily nature) drivers need to employ navigation skills to find the way to their destination. This can be easier if you have the help of a clued-up passenger, but otherwise safe and successful methods of route planning must be devised, which do not result in driver distraction (see page 120).

Routine journeys such as driving to and from work or taking the children to school are made more stressful by the frustration of being unable to make the desired progress at peak

times, resulting in a state of anxiety about whether one will arrive on time.

For people who drive as part of their daily job, there are the additional pressures of meeting deadlines – later in this book we shall consider the effects on business drivers of the need to arrive at a pre-arranged time, whatever the road and traffic conditions (see page 24). Fleet driver training is becoming recognised best practice, and most big companies now invest in further training.

The benefits of such training include:

- providing harassed employees with alternative strategies for managing their daily journeys and thereby improving personal safety

- employers seeing a reduction in injuries to staff (their most valuable asset) and in damage to company vehicles.

Investment in training by companies makes good economic sense, since the increase in insurance premiums when a driver has an accident is multiplied many times for an employer insuring a fleet of cars; so there are benefits both for the individual and for the company in keeping costs down. Some fleet insurers are even beginning to insist that companies they cover should invest in driver training.

In the course of this book we hope to make the case for undertaking further training in driving skills –

- whether for your own enjoyment and satisfaction, or at the request of your employer

- and whether you are a young or newly qualified driver, or a driver who passed the test many years ago, and are now looking to update your skills.

We shall encourage you to look more closely at the workings and capacity of your vehicle, and perhaps to expand your understanding of mechanical matters.

For those who want to understand more about the latest developments in technology, the choices available for in-car information and navigation systems are explained and assessed.

A panel of experts, including driving instructors who specialise in fleet driver training for AA The Driving School, have contributed their considerable range of experience to provide tips on all aspects of better driving. There are suggestions on how to spot visual clues to what's

happening ahead, how to maximise the benefits of road positioning, how to get the best from the car you drive, and much more.

At the end of each short section you'll find some questions to help check your understanding, and test your wider knowledge of qualified driver training skills. The answers at the back sometimes include additional relevant information which you may find useful.

Our aim is that by reading this book, in combination with undertaking some practical training in advanced driving skills, you will find that you become a more confident, more courteous, and above all a safer driver.

Advanced driving and you

More than 70,000 passengers in cars are injured every year.

Why people choose to undertake further training

In the first part of this book we look at some of the myths and realities about driving. We consider the reasons people give for undertaking further training; the importance of attitude in driving; the particular characteristics both of older drivers and of newly qualified drivers; and

the necessity for motorists to keep up with change.

Full licence holders who present themselves for further training fall into two broad categories:

● those who wish to improve their driving techniques for their own

interest and satisfaction, and/or a desire to become safer drivers

● and those who do so as a requirement of their job.

The first group can be characterised by the phrase 'driving for yourself' and the second by 'driving to comply with an employer's regulations'. But often, of course, the two will overlap. For example, an employee may seize enthusiastically upon the chance of undertaking driver training during work time and at his or her employer's expense, if the opportunity coincides with a personal awareness of a need to improve driving skills.

This awareness may arise at various significant points in a person's life; for example, when they change from being single to being married or living with a partner; or when children arrive on the scene, and drivers become more aware of responsibilities to people other than themselves. This can also apply to young drivers, who realise their shortcomings when friends are reluctant to be passengers in their car.

Driving is not an exact science, but it is rewarding to be able to do something important in life really well.

Lack of confidence can often strike in middle age for no apparent reason; many people complain of a feeling of claustrophobia in today's heavy traffic, and need to learn strategies for coping with it. Drivers who have been involved in accidents often request training to restore their confidence when out on the road. A wife (or husband) who has been widowed may find they need to drive far more than previously; in many cases they will have had little or no practice since passing their driving test long ago. Further training proves to be an empowering experience at a difficult time in life.

Any of these and many other motives may be present when an individual chooses to undertake further training;

BUT

● instructors will tell you from experience that frequently it is not those most in need of help who will volunteer for training!

Some health problems that make driving difficult, such as arthritis, can become less problematic after taking advice from an experienced instructor on adapting driving techniques.

Passing an 'advanced' driving test can be a good way to focus your desire to improve your driving, and can give a sense of heightened confidence on the road. However, it's important to remember that at the present time there is no single official or definitive test that certifies qualified driver training for the general public. (See also page 170.)

WHERE TO GO FOR QUALIFIED DRIVER TRAINING

A practical course in qualified driver training can bring back memories of techniques you were taught when you first learned to drive, and help you to look objectively at what you have taken for granted as the right way to drive over the years. The approach is non-judgmental, and there is no intention of 'showing you the error of your ways' – only of highlighting better or more efficient ways of doing things. You don't need to follow a certificated course or to sit an examination to improve your driving.

Having identified the need for training to improve your driving skills, where do you go to obtain it?

Perhaps the first question to ask yourself is how much time you wish (or are able) to set aside for training, and what sort of courses would appeal to you. You could choose training with an individual instructor who specialises in advanced driving; make sure that the instructor is a **qualified Approved Driving Instructor (ADI)** and has undertaken further appropriate training themselves.

Note: a fully qualified ADI has a **green badge** – if they have a **pink badge,** it means they are still in training themselves and cannot teach advanced driving. Do not accept training from anyone without a green badge.

A short overview of the style and content of the different options available follows here.

IAM

One of the best-known organisations offering courses in advanced driving techniques is the **Institute of Advanced Motorists (IAM)**. The IAM in the UK is organised into around 200 local groups, and there are also some groups overseas.

Courses usually involve structured tuition over several weeks, with a series of classroom lectures and practical sessions with an 'observer'. Specific advanced techniques are developed, and the organisation aims to promote a sense of responsibility and pride in good driving.

To take an IAM driving test you must hold a full UK or EC driving licence. The test can be taken in almost any vehicle of your choice, and drivers with disabilities are able to take the test if they have a suitably modified vehicle.

All IAM Examiners are holders of the Police Advanced Driving Certificate.

The test takes about 90 minutes and covers 35–40 miles, including all kinds of road conditions. Since 1956, when the IAM was founded, more than ¼ million people have taken the test, with a pass rate of around 70 per cent.

To contact the IAM, call **020 8994 4403,** or go to www.iam.org.uk.

RoSPA

The aim of the Royal Society for the Prevention of Accidents (RoSPA) is to promote safety at work and in all aspects of public life, including road safety. RoSPA has its own Advanced Drivers' Association, operating tests for cars, LGVs, motorcycles, minibuses and scooters. All RoSPA examiners are holders of the Police Advanced Driving Certificate.

Successful candidates are awarded a Gold, Silver or Bronze grade according to their level of competence.

To contact RoSPA, call **0121 248 2099,** or go to www.rospa.co.uk.

GEM

The Guild of Experienced Motorists (GEM) is a road safety association founded in 1932. GEM works closely with RoSPA to promote better driving standards and develop projects aimed at improving road safety. You can become a member as long as you have no recent convictions for serious motoring offences; you pay a subscription that entitles you to free motoring advice and access to GEM's breakdown/ recovery insurance scheme. Full members are those with ten years' driving experience or more, but you can join as an Associate member if you have less experience. You do not have to pass a test to join.

To contact GEM, call **01342 825676.**

DIAmond

The DIA is one of the largest professional associations for approved driving instructors in Britain, with a network of about 100 examiners around the country. The standard of its tests is high – six minor faults equals a fail – so extra tuition is advised if you want to pass their test, which is approved and monitored by the DSA. Successful candidates can join the MasterDriver Club, with access to its legal and domestic helplines.

To contact DIAmond, call **020 8660 3333,** or go to www.driving.org.

Police

The Police run qualified driver courses in some parts of the country, usually taught by former Grade 1 Police Driving Instructors. To find out whether tuition by police instructors is available in your area, contact your local police station.

Womens Motoring Service

The Womens Motoring Service provides support and information to women in the motoring industry, and runs a variety of courses including safer driving for 17-21 year olds and advanced driving tuition. (Men as well as women are welcome.) They also offer training on a skid pan, and organise track days and four-wheel drive events.

For further details, call **01483 810288** or go to www.womens-motoring .com.

Private companies

A number of private companies offer tuition, including ATC, Drivetech, Drive and Survive and NDI. More contacts can be found on the **Fleet Driver Training Association's** website: www.fdta.co.uk.

With the training given by the AA's Driving School, specially selected AA instructors give tuition. Before they begin delivering experienced driver training they must take a further training course themselves, so that they can adapt their approach and the content of their courses to people who have already passed the driving test, and whose needs and expectations are, of course, different from those of learner drivers. (And, unlike the Driving Test, there's no pass or fail.)

The **AA** is also actively involved in fleet driver training.Contact the AA's Driving School on **0800 607080.**

All companies offer a range of options, usually featuring a one-day awareness course supported by follow-up training; courses are customised for clients' requirements, and cover all types of vehicles. Reductions in the numbers of accidents following the course are regularly guaranteed – a company may even offer a free refresher course if a trainee has an accident for which they are to blame during the twelve months following their training course.

Some manufacturers, such as Lotus, have produced Track Day cars, which can be legally driven on the roads but are designed for 'fun' days out – rather like grown-up go-karts!

TRACK DAYS

If you sometimes feel frustrated about having no opportunity in normal driving to see how skilfully you could handle a car at really high speeds, why not consider saving up and booking a 'Track Day'?

Track days are held at many racing circuits around the country such as Castle Donington and Thruxton, and are run either by private racing schools or by the circuit owners. You can find out more information on the website of the **Association of Track Day Organisers**: www.atdo.co.uk.

There are also circuits within relatively easy reach abroad, such as the Nürburgring in Germany.

Safety is a high priority at track days, and anyone driving recklessly and endangering others will be asked to leave; no one is allowed to race any other person on the track. You can hire a car for the day or use your own (perhaps an exotic imported model?) to find out what it is really capable of and experience the thrill of speed well away from the public highway.

RALLY DRIVING

If you have an urge to experience the thrills of high-speed driving, then a one-day rally driving course provides a good way to channel it, while meeting fellow enthusiasts and enjoying the opportunity to compare vehicles.

Rallying is a sport where modified production cars are driven to the limit, using advanced techniques to make the cars move at a speed and in a manner that can seem to observers to defy the laws of physics. You can book a day to learn some of the techniques, such as controlling a rear-wheel drive car mainly on the throttle while using minimal steering – rather easier on mud than on tarmac.

To find out about rallying activities in your local area, check the website: www.ukmotorsport.com.

FOUR-WHEEL-DRIVING

Driving a four wheel-drive vehicle (4WD) demands different techniques from those for more conventional vehicles; a 4WD has a higher centre of gravity, and is more likely to topple over if you are forced to swerve, or drive too fast around a tight corner.

Taking a course in 4WD technique can greatly improve confidence in yourself and the vehicle, as you will learn about its capabilities and the range of obstacles it can overcome.

You will learn how to control the vehicle in different conditions, such as mud, deep water and steep hills, how to recover it if it gets stuck, and how the different gears and axle combinations work. After training you will be able to share the excitement of off-road driving with the family, by taking them to parts of the country inaccessible to standard vehicles.

If you own a 4WD or simply want to try one, check the off-road magazines for local clubs and tuition centres, or contact the **British Off Road Driving Association (BORDA)** website: www.borda.org.uk. One introduction to 4WD is Land Rover's 'Experience' course, based at its headquarters in Solihull; call **0121 700 4619,** or go to www.landrover.com. The Womens Motoring Service also provides rally-driving and 4WD training; see page 18 for contact details.

TEST YOUR UNDERSTANDING
OF THIS SECTION

1. What reasons do drivers give
    when deciding to undertake
    further training?

2. What options for tuition are
    available to you when you decide
    to enrol for a training course?

3. How does qualified driver
    training differ from the lessons
    provided for learner drivers?

Answers on pages 174–5

The right attitude

A person's attitude to risk-taking in general is likely to be reflected in their attitude to taking risks on the road.

Driving instructors are united in their view that attitude is all-important for safe driving.

Your frame of mind when you are behind the wheel affects not only you but also the other motorists whom you encounter; aggression on the part of one driver is quite likely to be countered by an aggressive response from others, and concentration is lost through focusing on the conflict.

> 'Anyone who, late for an appointment, tries to walk briskly along a crowded city street... will not improve his speed of progress if he angrily pushes aside his fellow-citizens, swears at them, or threatens them with physical assault. Yet this is precisely what a number of drivers in their vehicles do if pressed for time.'

Parry, M H, *Aggression on the Road*, London, Tavistock, 1968

Why do we find people who are perfectly reasonable in other aspects of their daily life behaving so aggressively when they are behind the wheel?

And if 'road rage' is a real phenomenon, why not 'pedestrian rage'?

Parry's comparison of walking with driving is an interesting one. Compared with walking, the act of driving is much more likely to give rise to anger and aggression.

- The very movement of walking can be relaxing, unlike the frustration of being confined in a car and unable to move forward.

- The risks of walking into someone on the street are minor compared to the risk of **damaging one's car** in a collision, and the resulting expense and inconvenience – let alone the human damage.

- Drivers are required to observe **externally imposed speed limits,** even though most cars are capable of exceeding them twice over. This 'levelling' effect can result in a temptation to use the vehicle to assert oneself through antisocial driving – demonstrated by such actions as tailgating and flashing headlights at a slower vehicle ahead. A great many drivers see their car as an extension of themselves, and the way they drive as an expression of their personality – although, of course, normally calm and placid people can change their personalities when they get behind the steering wheel!

Human beings are territorial, and anyone who invades our 'personal space' is seen as a threat. The car and the space around it is an extension of our 'territory', which we will instinctively 'defend' if someone encroaches on it. If another driver 'cuts in' we are tempted to re-establish our 'territory' by means of flashing lights, use of the horn, or chasing after the other driver. If you think about it, this is rather like an animal chasing away an attacker!

Understanding more about the way you behave in stressful situations makes it possible consciously to adjust your behaviour when driving – instinctive responses are common to everyone, but lives are lost when aggression between drivers is allowed to escalate.

Always remember:

● Expect the unexpected, and make provision for the potential errors of other drivers – everyone makes mistakes sometimes.

● Don't create unnecessary stress for other drivers by showing your frustration in an aggressive manner.

'Maintain eye contact with other drivers' is good advice, but it should be done positively and in a spirit of co-operation!

ATTITUDE, STRESS, AND THE BUSINESS DRIVER

People who drive for a living are under special pressures.

The prevailing culture of the workplace can all too often mean that staff are expected to arrive on time at their destination, whatever the road and traffic conditions; indeed, they may have to meet several such deadlines in the course of a day.

Road and rail

Compare the expectations of chaos for rail commuters, when it becomes impossible to predict what time a particular train will reach its destination – or whether it will run at all. Employers have had to come to terms with the fact that staff may phone with warnings of expected delays perceived as outside their control. But this flexibility does not always extend to employees travelling by road.

A young driver interviewed for a study by the **AA Foundation for Road Safety Research** had this to say:

'The company don't take travelling into account. They don't expect you to speed, but if you did [only] 50 miles an hour all the way they'd be upset. I'm so used to doing ridiculous speeds that it's second nature now. I'm expected onsite at 9am and they won't put you up in a hotel.'

The Foundation's response to this is that on a long journey, even one driven entirely on motorways, a driver who stays within the legal speed limits should expect an average speed of **no more than 55mph,** including stops. A mile a minute on A-class or lesser roads is simply an unreasonable expectation, and an employee on this schedule would have to drive much too fast to make up for time lost in a traffic tailback, or in following a slow-moving vehicle.

Other points to consider:

- Daily commuters who already get up early each morning don't always feel capable of allowing extra time to deal with the effects of, say, adverse weather conditions.

- As well as the sense of time ticking away while racing to an appointment, the business driver may have other anxieties on their mind, such as working out strategies and agendas for an important meeting. (See also 'Managing distractions', page 117).

All in all, this can add up to a sizeable package of assorted external pressures, which can in turn result in aggressive and higher-risk driving patterns.

Employers who invest in driver training programmes for their workforce have recognised these problems and are taking steps to do something positive about them, by providing an opportunity for their staff to look again at how they are driving, and identify those areas where they are taking too many risks and endangering themselves and others.

FOCUS ON HEALTH AND SAFETY

Another encouraging trend is seen in the **Government's Road Safety Strategy** initiative, entitled 'Tomorrow's Roads – Safer for Everyone' and launched by the Prime Minister in March 2000.

As a part of this, a **Health and Safety Executive Task Force** has been set up to identify the number of at-work accidents that happen on our roads, to make proposals for reducing them, and to define what more might be done to encourage employees to drive safely while at work.

Improving the driving skills of employees becomes part of an employer's responsibility for managing workplace health and safety, now that **the car is a place of work** for many people, much of the time.

About 15% of the 3,500 road accident deaths that happen every year involve people who are at work at the time of the accident.

25

TEST YOUR UNDERSTANDING
OF THIS SECTION

1. Why does the activity of driving often give rise to aggression?

2. What is meant by defensive driving?

3. What special pressures affect business drivers?

4. What are the key aims of the Road Safety Strategy in relation to post-test driver training?

Answers on pages 176–7

Keeping up with change

Think for a few moments about how much has changed since you learned to drive.

There have been

- changes to vehicles;

- changes to the driving test;

- changes in road conditions and traffic density (see pages 53–68);

- changes in recommended driving techniques from how these were taught in the past (see pages 77–86 and 95–108);

- and what about you as a driver? What changes have you noticed in yourself and how you approach road travel, since you first passed your test and became qualified to drive?

In any other practical skill, such as a sport or hobby, people expect to continually update their knowledge. Driving is no different, and should be seen as a whole-life skill, not one that starts and ends with your driving test.

There are simple techniques to help you park correctly and easily. If you hate parking in a confined space, why not book some tuition from an expert instructor?

THE PRACTICAL DRIVING TEST

How the Driving Test began

France was the first country to introduce a compulsory driving test, as long ago as 1893. Licensing existed in Britain from 1905, but only for the purposes of identification. *The Highway Code* was first published in 1931, but this had little effect on the mounting road death toll; in 1934 over 7,000 people were killed on the roads, although there were only 1½ million cars registered in Britain.

Compulsory testing began in Britain in 1935; at the same time the 30mph limit put in an appearance, along with Belisha beacons at pedestrian crossings (called after Leslie Hore-Belisha, who was Minister for Transport at the time).

Testing was suspended from 1939–46 due to World War II, and again during the Suez crisis of 1956, when learners were able to drive unaccompanied and examiners were drafted to help administer petrol rations. Formal testing of examiners was introduced in 1959.

In essence the test has changed little since 1935; the requirement to test arm signals was dropped in 1975, and reverse parking was added in 1991 (see below). Before the war most people got through on about 8–12 hours' tuition, and the pass rate was around 63 per cent; now most learners have 35 hours' tuition or more, combined with extra practice, and the average pass rate is 46 per cent, reflecting the far more hazardous conditions faced by drivers today.

Parking

Since 1991, parking has formed part of the test syllabus, and drivers who have qualified since that date will have been taught the techniques for reversing into a parking space successfully. 'Bay parking' is now carried out at certain test centres with suitable car parks. (*Note:* tips for the correct way to park are found on pages 95–6.)

Driving on different types of road

Recent changes have seen the length of the test extended to 40 minutes, to allow for inclusion of a wider range of road and traffic conditions. Part of the test is taken on faster roads, and more emphasis is placed on the whole art of driving, rather than on carrying out a series of manoeuvres.

Although the Driving Test routes do not currently extend to motorways (since learner drivers are not allowed on them), many learners now choose to book a lesson in motorway driving immediately after they pass their test in order to build up their skill and confidence. The AA's Driving School is one that provides this facility.

Highlighting the improvements to the test here is a way of demonstrating that older drivers, despite their experience, may be at a disadvantage in some ways, as they were not expertly taught all the skills that today's new drivers learn.

Of course, it is never too late to add to and revise your skills, and this is where experienced (or advanced) driver training has a key role.

Advanced driver training can be valuable in building your confidence about the best way to join fast-moving traffic on a motorway or dual carriageway. Those who learned to drive some time ago are often surprised to find that they were taught in ways no longer considered appropriate. One example is to turn and look back over your shoulder to check the blind spot – this is now seen as an unsafe habit when driving at speed, because you are looking away from the vehicle in front, and from the road ahead. The action now recommended by instructors is to glance to the side in order to check your blind spot, and use the mirrors to look into other areas.

THE THEORY TEST

The biggest single change to the Driving Test in recent years has been the introduction of an extra test, the **Theory Test.**

This has been in place since 1996, and learner drivers now have to pass both the Theory Test and the Practical Test in order to become qualified to hold a driving licence. In earlier times candidates attempted to learn *The Highway Code* by rote, so as to be able to answer the small number of questions posed by the examiner at the end of the test. The Theory Test demands more constructive thinking and a deeper knowledge and understanding of roadcraft.

The Theory Test consists of 35 multiple-choice questions, to be answered in 40 minutes using a touch-screen on a computer. The questions are selected from a bank of around one thousand, devised and held by the government agency, the Driving Standards Agency (DSA). New questions are regularly added to the bank and others, which have proved less useful, are removed.

The Highway Code **itself is now extremely comprehensive; if it is a while since you consulted it, obtain a current copy and take some time to read it through. The illustrations are particularly useful.**

Questions fall into the following broad range of categories:

- alertness
- attitude
- vehicle safety
- safety margins
- hazard awareness
- vulnerable road users
- other types of vehicles
- vehicle handling
- motorway rules
- rules of the road
- road and traffic signs
- documentation
- accidents
- vehicle loading.

Learner drivers must pass this test before applying for their Practical Test. The Practical Test must then be taken, and passed, within two years of passing the Theory Test.

It is interesting to note how trends in question-setting often mirror prime concerns in society; a notable example is the current prevalence of questions dealing with the use of mobile phones while on the move (see page 118).

If you learned to drive before the Theory Test was introduced, why not obtain a book of sample questions and see whether you can answer them? Choose one that has the up-to-date official questions from the DSA, such as the AA's *Driving Test Theory*. It's a good way of finding out how much has changed. For example, can you tell the difference between a pelican and a toucan crossing? Are you up to date with the latest advice on mobile phone use?

TEST YOUR UNDERSTANDING
OF THIS SECTION

1. What kind of knowledge must new drivers have in order to pass the Theory Test?

2. How is the Theory Test conducted?

3. Describe some recent changes to the content of the Practical Test.

Answers on page 178

You never stop learning

NEWLY QUALIFIED DRIVERS

Even though your Pass Certificate entitles you immediately to set out on any road including a motorway, drive a vehicle up to 3.5 tonnes and tow a small trailer, 'going solo' can be an alarming experience for newly qualified drivers.

The comforting presence of the instructor at your side is abruptly removed, and the responsibility for all decisions rests solely with you: decisions about whether to overtake or maintain your current position, whether to pull out or wait at a junction, and so on. You no longer have an L-plate to warn other drivers of your inexperience. You will also need to navigate as you go, instead of having directions relayed to you. (But losing the L-plate does have its advantages; some drivers regard an L-plate on a car as a justification for harassing and intimidating the car's driver.)

Most people react positively to the freedom to drive on their own. Problems can arise, however, when the enthusiasm of new drivers overrides their caution.

The key skills of anticipation, planning and space management develop steadily over time and new drivers must be prepared to make allowances for their own inexperience.

For example, research has shown that a newly qualified driver can be up to two seconds slower in spotting a potential hazard than someone with more experience.

Awareness will gradually improve until you can sense the full range of **hazards that may be building up outside your field of vision,** as well as those that are more immediately obvious. Use your eyes to look around more, and always keep your eyes moving.

It is important to acknowledge that you will inevitably make wrong judgments, from time to time, throughout your driving career; but your growing experience, backed up by voluntary further training at intervals, will mean that your reaction to any error will be faster and more effective in minimising risk to yourself and others.

Here are some points to bear in mind for the first few journeys after you pass your test:

Adapt your speed to the prevailing road and traffic conditions, but

- **don't feel pressured by other drivers** to drive at speeds faster than you are comfortable with.

There is nothing wrong with driving at a slightly slower speed than the one shown on the speed limit sign – it indicates a **limit, not a target.** (See box, page 46.)

In fact, it is often true that to drive at the top of the speed limit for certain roads could be positively dangerous: for example, on a country lane the national speed limit of 60mph may apply, but that would be completely inappropriate when negotiating a blind bend.

- **Don't feel pressured by friends** to drive in a showy or unsafe manner. Remember, you don't have anything to prove; after all, you have passed your test.

Research has shown that young male drivers are the group most at risk,

and that risk increases when they have another young male as a passenger. (However, sometimes it can be your passengers' reluctance to ride with you that brings home to you your need to improve your driving! – see page 15.)

So, put any thoughts of impressing others with flashy driving firmly out of your mind, and

drive with tomorrow in mind – not just today.

- Try to **watch out for a tendency to develop bad driving habits** once you are through the test.

- Train yourself to **anticipate corners** – think ahead for what may be around the corner, such as a cyclist, and don't leave braking until the corner is upon you.

- Where **overtaking** is concerned, make consistent efforts to improve your judgment.

- Take **extra care at junctions** – don't be in too much of a hurry to pull out, it is better to incur the impatience of the driver behind than to risk an accident. After all, you are in the best position to decide whether it is really safe to move out. Don't rely on the signals of other road users – make

An experienced driver is one who copes better with mistakes – their own and other people's.

Statistics show that accidents are caused not by high speeds alone, but by speeds that are inappropriate for the road and traffic conditions.

A high proportion of accidents to newly qualified drivers happen on 'quiet' country roads where no other vehicle is involved – because they are going too fast, drivers often lose control and veer off the road, perhaps hitting a tree, or ending up in the ditch.

sure **you are certain** of where they are going.

Other ways in which new drivers can help themselves to improve are listed on the following page.

P-plates

Newly qualified drivers have the option of displaying a green P-plate for a period of time after they have passed their test. (The 'P' stands for Probationer.)

P-plates are not a legal requirement in England, Scotland and Wales, though their use has become more widespread.

Note: In Northern Ireland, an orange R-plate must be displayed for 12 months after passing your test, and your speed must not exceed 45mph on any road.

However it is regrettably true that some drivers regard the P-plate, like the L-plate, as a target.

Whether you decide to display a P-plate is of course a matter for individual choice, but perhaps the best approach is to start as you mean to go on:

drive with confidence and care, actively seeking ways to improve your driving skills from Day 1.

OTHER WAYS TO IMPROVE YOUR SKILLS

- Remember the importance of **planning your route.** Before you set out on a long journey, or even on a short journey if it is to an unfamiliar destination, write down a clear and readable list of the major towns along the route, and instructions to yourself of how you will proceed at complex roundabouts and junctions. If you prefer, tape your route directions and play them back as you drive.

Plan an **alternative route** in case your intended one doesn't work out (because of roadworks, accidents, weather conditions etc).

- If you don't already know how to use **grid references** on maps, find out; always use a good, clear and up-to-date road atlas. (However, don't expect to read the map as you drive.)

- If you are travelling at a peak time and feel unsure about your ability to cope with the demands of a busy motorway, choose a parallel **A-road** instead.

(For more on route planning, see pages 154–6.)

- Use *The Highway Code* to familiarise yourself with the signs you'll encounter on the motorway, and check the procedure for dealing with breakdowns.

- Further training can open your eyes to the full range of information that you're taking in and processing all the time when you're on the road.

Even the most seemingly boring stretch of road has a great deal to tell you. You can find out just how much by practising **commentary driving.**

Take a tip from the AA's qualified driver instructors, and try commentary driving to increase your observation and awareness and improve your concentration. Talk to yourself as you drive, pointing out hazards you can see ahead and making decisions about how you will react to them. (See also page 56.)

If your vision is worse at night, this is due to the rod-shaped light receptors in your retina not working properly. This can happen as people get older, but is also caused by lack of vitamin A in the diet or by the inherited eye condition *retinitis pigmentosa*. (See also page 127.)

OLDER DRIVERS

We move on to consider the situation of the ever-increasing numbers of older drivers on our roads.

The **AA Foundation for Road Safety Research** has commissioned several research projects on this topic, and their work concerning older drivers is considered the most important long-term study yet produced in this field.

Consider these statistics:

- At the time of writing almost 15 million of the UK's population are over 55 years old, and 4.2 million are 75 and over. By 2031 it is expected there will be nearly 22.5 million people over 55, and 6.7 million who are 75 and over.

- In 1975 only 33% of men and 4% of women aged 70 and over held driving licences; by 1997 this had risen to 65% and 22%.

- A survey in 1997 of the 40–49 age group showed 89% of men and 74% of women hold licences. Most, or all of these, presumably intend to continue driving for many years.

The trend for longevity, coupled with increased affluence and increasing numbers of women learning to drive, gives a good indication of the likely age profile of the driver population in years to come.

How good are older drivers?

Does the increasing number of older drivers represent a cause for concern? Is it likely to result in more accidents? The answers may surprise you.

Research by the Department of the Environment, Transport and the Regions (DETR) suggests that the following qualities are necessary for driver safety:

- muscle strength
- balance
- good vision
- good hearing.

However, even where these abilities are somewhat diminished, it does not follow that the driver will be unsafe; only that people with keen eyesight and hearing do rather better. When someone is aware that they may have a problem, they will usually drive more carefully. This particularly applies in the case of people with poor night vision – they actually have fewer accidents, because they are **taking more care.**

As an expert driver, you should be aware that some older drivers have difficulty in assessing speed and distance, and adjust your driving when necessary.

Older drivers and self-regulation

In a study comparing older drivers who had decided they would give up driving at a certain age and those who had not, the people who had not even considered giving up driving were generally fitter and had better safety records.

If older people dislike driving in the dark, they avoid doing so. If they don't feel comfortable driving on long journeys, they will find an alternative means of getting to their destination.

They may choose to avoid routes involving busy junctions, or driving in city centres or during the rush hour.

Generally, older people are very responsible about driving. Their main strength is that **they have learned to regulate themselves.**

In the US state of Illinois, a long-term health-screening program for older drivers was discontinued as an experiment when no discernible effect on driver safety was found.

The decision to stop driving

Some older people decide not to drive after a certain age; for some people, the prospect of tests and medical examinations is sufficient reason (see 'Re-testing for older drivers', page 171).

However, the car is essential to many older people's lifestyles, and to suggest that a person is too old to drive can cause great anxiety.

Another consideration is the issue of **pedestrian deaths** among elderly people – 'the forgotten problem of British road safety'. Pedestrians over the age of 60 account for 450 deaths a year; almost half of all pedestrian deaths.

It is possible that by forcing older drivers to give up driving, more older people could be at risk, when drivers and their passengers become pedestrians at risk.

Driver improvement training for older drivers

The findings about the general fitness and competence of older drivers are certainly very

encouraging; but no one would deny that there are ways in which they can benefit from some specialist training.

- People who have been driving for many years, especially those who frequently use the same routes, can have a tendency to drive as if 'on autopilot', and are thus at risk of missing potential hazards.

- They may have got into bad habits, for example:

  crossing hands on the wheel (see page 84)

  changing all the way down through the gears, instead of using the procedure now considered correct (see page 80)

  resting one arm on the window-ledge or armrest, or on the gear lever, instead of keeping both hands on the wheel.

- Those older people who began driving before 1935 – when the Driving Test was introduced – may exhibit bad habits because they were never taught differently. For example, it was once considered good manners, when turning right off a busy road, to pull over to the left and let traffic pass before moving to the right.

- Accident records reveal one area where older drivers are represented especially highly – *accidents at road junctions.*

It seems that these drivers have particular problems with **right turns,** and with junctions at **oblique angles.**

This is one instance where a course of tuition could restore confidence and judgment, and encourage better technique.

- **Reversing skills** may also deteriorate with increasing age.

The problem is not so much with driving ability, but with being able to look in the direction you wish to go – due to decreased flexibility in the neck and spine.

Consider this:

decisions about how we drive in retirement will almost certainly be made while we are still working.

How easy or difficult is it for a person to adapt the way they drive in retirement, after a working life 'on the road'?

Try to turn round in your seat and look well back up the road. If you find you are looking at the hedge at the roadside, you are likely to end up in it!

TEST YOUR UNDERSTANDING
OF THIS SECTION

1. How can people who have just passed their test benefit from further training?

2. In what ways are experienced drivers more competent at hazard awareness than newly qualified drivers?

3. In what situations are drivers most likely to exceed the speed limit?

4. What are the pros and cons of using P-plates?

5. What advance preparations can be used to result in more successful journeys?

6. What reasons are given for the increased numbers of older drivers on our roads?

7. Are older people better or worse drivers than younger people?

8. What are some examples of bad habits in driving?

Answers on page 179–80

Understanding risk

Most people are conscious of taking a risk every time they get behind the wheel of a car. It is of course pointless to dwell on this too much, it would become impossible to face making your necessary day-to-day journeys; on the other hand, a healthy awareness of risk is necessary to ensure concentration at all times.

HIGH-RISK DRIVING SITUATIONS

Driving instructors agree that there are some driving situations that are particularly risky, especially:

● road junctions, and other areas where traffic merges

● manoeuvres that involve reversing

● driving at high speeds.

ROAD JUNCTIONS

A high proportion of accidents occur at junctions, because two or more vehicles are aiming to proceed along the same stretch of road.

Note: for a reminder of the main types of junctions and the road signs that warn you what to expect in each case, see the next page.

An accident, however, does not simply 'happen'; it results from an error of judgment on the part of one or more drivers – 96% of accidents are caused by **people.** Part of becoming an expert driver is being able to anticipate the risks at crossroads and junctions, roundabouts and motorway slip roads, so that you can take appropriate action and proceed in safety.

It is also very important **not to make any assumptions** about how other drivers will proceed.

An accident between vehicles can be summed up as: when two drivers try to occupy the same space at the same time.

When judging the probable actions of another vehicle at a junction, check for clues such as the position on the road of the opposing vehicle and the angle of the wheels.

For example:

When turning left **at a T-junction,** you may see a vehicle approaching from the right with the left indicator flashing. It would not be safe to pull out on the basis of that signal alone, since it could have been left on in error; or the driver may actually intend to pull in to the left further on; or they may change their mind at the last minute, and continue straight on what then becomes a collision course with your vehicle.

A high risk of accidents also occurs **at an unmarked crossroads,** where no vehicle has priority.

These crossroads may be found in older housing estates, or in rural locations, where you are further at risk due to poor visibility caused by high verges or blind bends on both sides – especially when you want to proceed straight across.

Approaching another vehicle at an unmarked crossroads, look for clues to work out where the other driver intends to go, if signalling is not clear. For example, are the wheels turned in any way? Is the driver looking in the direction they intend to go? If you are unsure, **slow down** and wait until the intention of the other driver becomes clear.

Correct sig-
nalling is vital.
Many accidents
result from dri-
vers not
signalling; or
signalling too
soon (for exam-
ple, before
turning left); or
giving a signal
that is mislead-
ing.

Can you be too courteous?

Part of being an expert driver consists of being able to judge when it is both courteous and safe to let another driver go first, and when the right course of action is for *you* to go first and leave the road clearer for others.

You are causing a risk if, for example, you wave to someone to turn out of a junction which results in drivers behind you having to brake.

You should never wave pedestrians on to a crossing, as you cannot be sure that oncoming drivers will stop, or drivers behind you will not overtake illegally on the pedestrian crossing and cause an accident.

You should only tell other drivers, by means of your signals, what **you** intend to do; you should not attempt to make decisions for other drivers, by flashing your lights or waving them on.

Although flashing headlights are often used by drivers to indicate to others that they are letting them go first, it can be most alarming to discover, when driving in other countries, that the flashing lights often mean just the opposite – namely, 'I am coming through'!

(See page 100 for more detailed advice about how to avoid accidents at junctions.)

Use positive
and effective
eye contact to
achieve a safe
resolution of
the question of
who goes first.

Where reversing is concerned, those most at risk from drivers' mistakes are likely to be pedestrians – especially elderly people and children.

REVERSING MANOEUVRES

Many accidents occur as a result of drivers **not paying sufficient attention** to approaching traffic, or carrying out the manoeuvre **too fast**, so that they do not have adequate control of the car.

Older drivers can be more at risk when reversing because of decreased flexibility in the neck and spine (see page 39).

Note: the law allows drivers to remove their seat belt temporarily if this helps them to reverse more safely.

The Highway Code gives clear guidance about the right way to reverse, including:

- choosing a safe place for the manoeuvre

- avoiding reversing in busy roads, or near school entrances and children's play areas

- making use of all mirrors, and checking all round for pedestrians as well as other vehicles

- looking out for obstructions behind you (such as a concrete marker post in a car park)

- looking mainly through the rear window.

Other tips include getting someone to help you if you cannot see clearly all round, or if you unavoidably have to reverse into a busy situation; and driving round the block, if it will save you from carrying out a potentially dangerous manoeuvre. If in doubt, get out and walk to the rear of the car to look behind.

Always reverse from the road into a driveway – not from the driveway into the road. Whenever possible reverse into a parking bay – for example, at a supermarket car park – because it is safer and easier to exit forwards.

Note: if your rear view is limited by your vehicle's design or your own height, consider attaching a **reversing mirror** to your rear window to improve visibility. (See also 'Parking', page 95.)

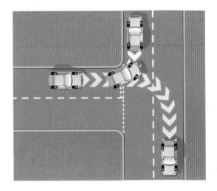

DRIVING AT SPEED

Speed in itself is not risky. Driving at speed along a clear stretch of road on a fine day is one of the pleasures of motoring; and expert drivers will confirm the satisfaction that comes from giving your car an opportunity to show its best performance.

But most roads in the UK are too crowded with traffic for you to drive safely at high speed.

Accidents can be caused by:

driving above the legal speed limit

and

driving too fast for the road and traffic conditions.

Note: ever year, over 130 children die and more than 4,500 are seriously injured while walking and cycling.

There is among drivers a **great disregard for speed limits.** Opinion polls have shown that although most people believe that causing death by drinking and driving is a serious crime, many do not regard breaking the speed limit as a criminal act at all.

- In a survey taken in 1998, 69% of drivers exceeded the 30mph limit and 29% exceeded the 40mph limit (in free-flowing traffic).

- Research by psychologists at the University of Reading has shown that people select the speed they will drive at by weighing up the possible costs (being fined, losing licence points) against the benefits (arriving in a shorter time).

- Many drivers seem to work on the basis that it is safe to exceed the limit shown by around 10mph.

Speed cameras

Many drivers deal with these by slowing down within the camera's range, then rapidly picking up speed.

However, ways of trapping speeding motorists are becoming more sophisticated. Digital cameras, which do not flash, are being introduced, making it difficult to gamble on the camera having no film. Sometimes cameras are used to record your average speed over a given distance, with the second camera trapping offenders. And you could find that the innocuous-looking car behind contains a police officer tracking your speed along a motorway or dual carriageway.

Note: in many cities, traffic lights are now equipped with built-in cameras to catch offenders who 'jump' the lights.

Unofficially, police may allow a margin of up to 10% over the limit, to allow for speedometers that are not always accurate; so driving at 34mph in a 30mph zone can still result in a fine and loss of points on your licence.

Speed is a major contributory factor in about one-third of all road accidents.

Watch carefully for speed limits marked on the road – not just on traffic signs.

Why do we need so many speed limits?

- Residents of villages have been so concerned about the risks caused by speeding motorists that they have campaigned successfully for 30mph limits to begin and end **well outside the village boundaries.**

- **Traffic calming measures** have also been introduced to combat the risks caused by speed in residential areas; make sure you know about the latest kinds.

Understanding the reasons for speed limits, and respecting them when you see them, is all part of expert driving.

Don't forget that driving too slowly for the conditions can also be risky:

- it causes frustration for other motorists

- it encourages drivers behind to overtake when they cannot see clearly ahead.

Driving at a speed where you are comfortable is quite acceptable (see page 33) – but that speed should not be so far below the limit as to make you a serious obstacle to other legitimate road users.

HIGH-RISK TIMES AND PLACES

To anyone who has just passed their driving test, the size and speed of **motorways** can seem dangerous and frightening.

However, the safety record for motorways (and high-speed dual carriageways as well) is better than that for smaller, **urban roads** – the place where the largest number of accidents occur.

There are many reasons for this:

- traffic moving only in one direction

- fewer hazards – for example, no pedestrians, cyclists, animals, low-speed vehicles, etc

- used by more experienced drivers who know how to anticipate and deal with hazards

- higher quality road surface.

By contrast, the most dangerous streets for drivers and pedestrians alike are **town or village high streets**.

Hazards found in urban areas include:

- frequent junctions, mini-roundabouts and traffic-lights

- pedestrian crossings, with or without lights

- bus lanes and perhaps tram lanes

- roadworks that slow your progress

- stationary vehicles, perhaps illegally parked, and other obstructions such as delivery vans, necessitating overtaking with poor visibility.

You must also be on the watch for slower pedestrians, children suddenly running out into the road, or dogs that are not on leads.

Most people think that they are less likely to have an accident than the average driver. Remember that road safety awareness campaigns concern you – not only other people.

About 4% of accidents occur on motorways compared with 70% in urban areas.

47

Times of day

Obviously there are some times of the day that are much busier than others. If you travel at peak times, you need to be prepared for some delays (such as waiting for a bus in front to move off), and to be aware of other vehicles joining from side roads or turning off.

A different kind of risk applies when the high street is relatively quiet – the risk of exceeding the speed limit, or of driving across a zebra crossing without checking whether there are pedestrians waiting to cross.

Times when parents are either **driving or walking their children to school** present perhaps the greatest risks. Drive with extra care in the vicinity of the school, and be prepared to stop for school crossing patrols.

School holidays and public holidays usually mean less traffic on urban roads (though more on the motorways), but drivers must still be on their guard – perhaps for drivers venturing on to the road who do so only infrequently and who may behave unpredictably, or for drivers not showing sufficient concentration because they are not expecting to meet other vehicles. Cutting corners, taking bends too fast, and even straying on to the wrong side of the road – these are all instances of the wrong kind of 'holiday mood'.

Later on we look at **high-risk driving conditions,** for example adverse weather, and the risks that result from **fatigue and stress.** (See pages 128–30.)

But to conclude this section on understanding risk, we look briefly at **different types of vehicles** and how they score in safety assessments; and also at how the **characteristics** of your vehicle can **affect the way you drive.**

CHOOSING A VEHICLE
People, not vehicles, cause accidents

However, it is worth considering the safety reports published by consumer magazines when choosing a car. They can advise how the model you're thinking of buying is likely to perform in an accident, and what safety features the manufacturers have incorporated to protect the driver, the passengers and also any pedestrians near the scene.

Euro NCAP

The European New Car Assessment Programme publishes comparative reports on different makes of vehicles, in categories such as 'small family cars' or 'people-carriers'.

They work in partnership with motoring organisations in Europe, including the AA, and also with the Alliance Internationale de Tourisme (AIT), the Federation Internationale de l'Automobile (FIA), and other consumer and road safety organisations.

NCAP grades cars according to a five-star rating system, judging how the vehicles perform in test simulations for:

- side impact collisions

- front impact collisions

- risk of injury to driver

- risk of injury to passengers

- risk of injury to pedestrians.

The reports look at how well different parts of the body, such as the **head** and **legs,** are protected by the car's design, and whether adequate **seat belts, airbags** and **child restraints** have been included.

Cars score highly if they have fully integrated, adjustable child restraints built in. If the manufacturer does not include these but recommends a particular make of child restraint, these should be capable of being firmly held in place by the seat belts.

The vehicles are also assessed for the risks they pose to **pedestrians:** focusing on the bonnet leading edge, the bumper and (worst of all) 'bull bars' if fitted. If you are hit by a vehicle fitted with a bull bar and travelling at 20mph, it's equivalent to being hit by a vehicle travelling at twice that speed, because the bull bars are unyielding and not curved like car bonnets.

Bearing in mind that in a high proportion of accidents (especially to new drivers) only one vehicle is involved, the tests now look at safety features targeting **side impact**

A recurring problem has been the danger of using a front passenger airbag in combination with a rear-facing child restraint. In a collision, the airbag could crush the child as it inflates. All vehicles should now carry clear warnings.

collisions with stationary objects (such as telegraph poles). Side airbags with a 'curtaining' effect have been introduced in some cars to improve safety.

The constant amendments to car design, which are being made by manufacturers, have done much to improve safety records, and cut down the number of collisions that result in deaths. But it is important that this should not result in a corresponding increase in **complacency among drivers** (see next page).

What NCAP tests tell us about collisions and pedestrian injuries

The most common types of collisions are front-to-rear; the most serious are front-to-front collisions. However, **injuries** resulting from side impact crashes are usually more serious; Euro NCAP tests focus on the driver's side, where there is added risk of injury from the steering wheel and the pedals. Tests are designed to replicate as accurately as possible exactly what might happen in an accident in a wide variety of vehicles.

Most **pedestrians** injured in accidents are hit by the front of the vehicle. Euro NCAP tests assess how well various cars measure up to standards of minimising risk to pedestrians – whether the front of the car is stiff and unforgiving, or good at absorbing and cushioning the impact.

The key impact areas are the bumper (lower leg), the leading edge of the bonnet (upper leg), the rest of the bonnet up to the windscreen (about the height of a child's head) and the windscreen itself (adult head).

SEATBELT SAFETY

Full three-point seat belts are much safer than the static lap belts found in the centre back seat of some cars.

- The lap strap of the seatbelt should rest over your thighs, not your stomach. Pull upwards on the shoulder strap to remove any slack.

- For maximum safety when using a centre rear seat lap belt, the passenger should sit well back, with the belt comfortably tight.

AIRBAG SAFETY

- When sitting in the driver's seat your chest bone should be not less than 250mm from the airbag cover. If this is not the case, move or recline the seat back.

- **Never** allow a passenger to sit with their feet resting in the area of the passenger's airbag. If the bag inflates, it could cause severe injury to the back and spine.

- **Never** fit a rear-facing child restraint in a seat with a frontal airbag. The inflating bag will crush the child against the back of the seat.

- **Never** smoke with an airbag in front of you – if the airbag inflates, a cigarette or pipe will be pushed down your throat.

- **Never** cross your hands on the steering wheel or hold on to the inside of the wheel – the impact of the airbag inflating is liable to smash your arm into your face.

VEHICLE CHARACTERISTICS

Have you ever thought about the fact that the sort of car you choose might have an effect on the way you drive?

Researchers have carried out several experiments to find out whether:

fast cars cause people to drive fast – or fast drivers choose to buy fast cars.

The results show that the first of these is true – owning a fast car encourages faster driving.

It may also encourage risk-taking; for example, knowing you have plenty of acceleration available can lead you to aim your car into ever-smaller gaps when overtaking.

Here are some other ways in which it has been shown that your car can influence your driving:

- If your car's engine is very quiet, you will tend to drive faster. Loud engine noise discourages drivers from speeding.

- When anti-lock brakes are fitted, people tend to drive more riskily because they assume they are protected. This includes driving too close to the car in front, and driving too fast in icy conditions.

In all these cases, the protective effect of the safety features is counteracted by the way the owner chooses to drive.

Safety features do not equal invulnerability.

Note: the factor proved to be most effective in causing people to change their driving behaviour is **being involved in accident where they were (or thought they were) to blame.** Researchers have found that showing a video of a serious accident and asking people to imagine they were to blame is just as effective.

If you own a people-carrier, remember that the risk of injury increases when the vehicle is fully loaded with up to seven passengers plus luggage.

TEST YOUR UNDERSTANDING
OF THIS SECTION

1. Which driving situations are especially risky?

2. Drivers sometimes show 'inappropriate courtesy'. Give some examples of this.

3. What should you bear in mind when reversing your vehicle?

4. Why do some motorists regularly ignore speed limits?

5. When can it be risky to drive slowly?

6. Are you more likely to have an accident when driving on:

   a) a motorway?

   b) a high street in a town?

   Give reasons.

7. How can you best ensure the safety of children who travel in your car?

8. How might your choice of car affect your driving?

Answers on pages 181–2

Reading the road

Reading the road

Here we look at techniques you can put into practice to help you become a better driver.

This section focuses on the four key aspects that are covered in the AA's Fleet Driver Training courses:

- **hazard perception**
- **observation**
- **anticipation**

and

- **planning.**

Expert driving instructors also identify two further important skills:

- **space management**

and

- **communication.**

Hazard perception

The Government's Road Safety strategy stresses the vital importance of hazard perception skills for all drivers, and especially of improving these skills in the case of newly qualified drivers. One initiative is the move to **introduce digitised video clips of driving hazards as part of the Theory Test,** to help in testing topics such as motorway driving.

Note: the DSA's video and booklet, *What If?,* are an excellent visual aid to hazard awareness, anticipation and planning – a valuable aid for any expert driver.

What is a hazard?

● A hazard is anything that may cause you to change course or alter your speed.

It could be a vehicle pulling out ahead of you, or turning out of a junction without waiting; a car from behind overtaking and then cutting in, forcing you to slow down; a cyclist on a narrow road, whom you must follow at very low speed; or a child running out into the road, causing you to stop abruptly. You have to be constantly on your guard, 'expecting the unexpected', and making decisions with the aim of ensuring safety for yourself and other road users, especially those who are most vulnerable.

Hazard perception is closely linked with the other key skills of **observation, anticipation and planning.**

The 'Hazard Awareness' section of the AA's *Driving Test Theory* book is a good place to find examples of a wide range of hazards encountered by drivers – many questions have colour illustrations, with arrows indicating the potential hazards.

Our eyes can transmit 30 to 40 images per second; the problem lies in how we interpret these images, and how we act on the information.

Commentary driving

Commentary driving is recommended by advanced driving instructors as a way of teaching yourself to look farther ahead and consciously note road and traffic hazards that may be building up (see page 35). If you practice reciting a 'running commentary' on what you see around you and ahead (and behind you in the mirrors), you will find that you start to notice more potential hazards, and your ability to process visual input improves.

Imagine that you are driving along a busy high street in a town. Your 'running commentary' might go something like this:

- Pedestrian crossing controlled by lights; *observe any pedestrians approaching the crossing; slow down, change gear and be prepared to stop; if lights still flashing, give way to pedestrians, otherwise proceed.*

- Bus stationary in bus lay-by ahead; *it may pull out; there may be pedestrians shielded by the bus, trying to cross the road; observe any signals.*

- Bus not moving; *no need to indicate, carry on.*

- Small child near edge of pavement, shopping with parent; *is the child holding its parent's hand?*

- Roadworks for cable laying; traffic controlled by person with 'STOP/GO' sign; *watch out for other drivers speeding to get through before the sign changes.*

- Small dog with owner; *is it on a lead, or is it likely to run into road?*

- Now approaching roundabout at end of high street; *am I in the correct lane for my destination?*

As part of your driver training course your instructor may demonstrate a commentary drive, then invite you to have a go yourself. You will be able to add to the list of examples of hazards given above – drivers are constantly engaged in decision-making about how to deal with events ranging from routine delays to 'one-off' accidents.

You should gain a greater awareness of being correctly positioned on the road (keeping to the left but not too close in to the kerb), and learn to focus attention on the traffic coming towards you and how you need to react to it. At the same time you will be regularly checking your mirrors for traffic approaching from behind.

You will also learn to recognise what kinds of things might become hazards, as well as those which are already evident.

Some driver training courses give you an opportunity to test your level of hazard perception by using video; you are shown a traffic scene filmed from the driver's point of view, and you press a button whenever you think something dangerous is about to happen on the screen.

Research into hazard perception by psychologists at the University of Reading has produced two interesting conclusions:

● Most skills become increasingly automatic with practice, but this doesn't apply to hazard perception. Experienced drivers actually put **more** effort into reading the road ahead, because their experience has taught them how much they need to be on the lookout for hazards. Novice drivers on the other hand tend just to react to situations, rather than reading the road far enough ahead to allow time to react and deal with a hazard in good time.

● If you have to concentrate on another task at the same time as driving – such as carrying on a

conversation with a passenger, or deciding which route to follow – your reaction time to hazardous situations slows right down. This proves the importance of maintaining continuous concentration; do not allow yourself to be distracted while driving (see 'Managing distractions', page 117).

Improving your skill in hazard perception through training can have a positive effect on:

● the time you take to react to potential dangers

● the speed you choose to drive at

and it will also result in your taking fewer risks in the future.

With most skills, young people's reaction times are faster than older people's. But with driving, the people who have the earliest reactions to dangerous situations are those aged about 50. However, training can successfully compensate for lack of experience.

TEST YOUR UNDERSTANDING
OF THIS SECTION

1. What effect do age and experience have on hazard perception?

2. How can you use the technique of 'commentary driving' to improve your standard of driving?

3. How are video clips used in training drivers to spot hazards?

4. List some potential hazards you might encounter when driving.

Answers on page 183

Observation

Linked to **hazard perception** is **observation,** and the ability to look well ahead in order to decide on the appropriate response to any traffic situation.

Use the technique of commentary driving (see page 56) to describe what you see; this will highlight the hazards you have previously missed.

SCANNING

- Look **as far ahead as possible,** and **aim high.** A good technique is to glance to the horizon as each new view opens up. This may only be to a building at the end of the road, or a much longer view on a country road. It will provide a snapshot of what's coming up; you can then give your attention to those points you prioritise as hazards. You should be looking at least 15 seconds ahead, and up to 30 seconds ahead in some situations such as motorways and main roads in towns.

- Train yourself to scan as much as possible within your field of vision, using all three mirrors, and scanning the area from distant to near. Try also to be aware of hazards building up just outside your field of vision.

- Avoid **fixing** your eyes on one point; use your **peripheral vision.**

- Become familiar with the **blind spot** in your field of vision while driving, and find safe ways of checking all around for hazards. Remember that you have a blind spot on the left as well as the right.

Make an extra effort to be observant when you feel tired, or when you have been driving for a long time. If you travel the same route daily, don't let familiarity dull your observation.

59

Your senses of hearing and smell are, of course, just as important for alerting you to problems inside your vehicle as well as outside – see page 148.

Remember that sunlight and shadows can play tricks with your eyesight, and it can be difficult to see clearly ahead (or in your mirrors) when the sun is low in winter. Twilight driving can make it difficult to judge distances of other vehicles; and you are likely to be less observant when you are tired (see 'Driving at night and dealing with tiredness', page 127).

Using your observation skills – some examples

Effective observation involves taking note of everyday events and interpreting them, so that you can tell which ones are likely to develop into hazards.

FOR EXAMPLE:

● a ball bouncing across the road:

  suggests a child may run out after it

● dustbins or rubbish bags put out on the pavement:
  you may soon have to slow for a dustcart, or operatives crossing the road with rubbish

● people waiting for a bus on your left:

  the bus may appear, and other pedestrians may be hurrying across the road

● you see an incurving (deflection) arrow marked on the road surface ahead:

  it is not safe to overtake from this point

● you see an inverted triangle marked on the road surface ahead:

  this sign warns you of a 'Give Way' just ahead

- a vehicle with lights flashing appears in your rear view mirror:

  you may need to take action to allow an emergency vehicle to pass.

This last example can be used to illustrate another point about observation –

   it involves more than just your sense of sight.

FOR EXAMPLE:

- you might **hear** a hedge cutter around the corner in a country lane, or even smell the grass cuttings

- you might **smell** burning rubber, which could give warning of a vehicle with a burst tyre

- you may **hear** the siren of an emergency vehicle before you see it.

If you hear the siren of an emergency vehicle, try to define which direction it is approaching from, so you can act in good time if necessary. This can be difficult in built-up areas, where the sound bounces off buildings, masking the true direction.

The examples above are interpretations of fairly obvious signs, but you should also look harder for clues that are more cryptic.

- On a narrow street of parked cars, look in the door mirror of each vehicle for the presence of a driver, to assess the risk of a door opening or a vehicle pulling out.

- A flash of brake lights from a parked vehicle ahead means the door may open, or the vehicle may move off.

- A puff of smoke from the exhaust of a parked vehicle ahead means the vehicle will move soon, possibly just before, or maybe just after you have passed. (A puff of exhaust is not easy to see – you must be looking.)

- A passenger standing up in the aisle of a bus you are following means the bus will stop soon, so you should prepare to brake or overtake.

TEST YOUR UNDERSTANDING
OF THIS SECTION

1. How does 'scanning' differ from 'looking'?

2. When should you make an extra effort to be observant?

3. If you noticed a pile of black rubbish sacks at the edge of the road, what would you expect to see next?

4. What kinds of information can you get from markings on the road?

5. Explain how and why you need to use all your senses as part of your observation technique.

Answers on page 184

Anticipation and planning

Being able to make a good guess at what is likely to happen next in any given situation is part of being an expert driver.

You have to rely a good deal on **instinct** and **intuition** – and learn how to be **proactive** instead of **reactive.**

(Compare this with the tendency of novice drivers to be mainly reactive – see page 32.)

You also have to allow for the fact that **others may make mistakes.**

'POSITION FOR VISION'

Advanced driving instructors emphasise the importance of taking up a position on the road that will enable you to **see as far ahead** as it is possible to do safely, and to **assess** what is approaching and from what direction.

You should also make sure that your position enables drivers coming towards you to have plenty of time to see you.

An example of 'position for vision' is to keep well over to the left at a

Your driving instructor may have taught you this tip: **MSM–PSL,** which stands for **Mirror–Signal–Manoeuvre, Position–Speed–Look.**

1

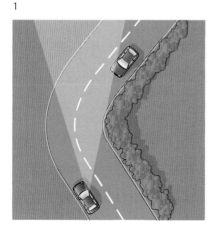

2

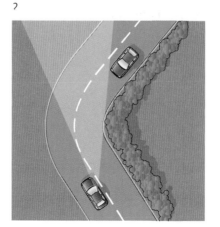

Another instructor's tip: 'Early vision – easy decision!'

3

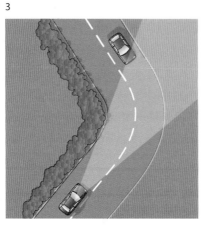

4

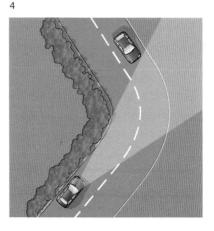

right-hand bend (as far as it is safe to do so). This will:

- improve your view of the road ahead – that is, you can see as far ahead as it is possible to do

- improve the view that other drivers have of you – in other words, drivers coming towards you have longer to see you

- and enable you to make the right decision on how to proceed.

The diagrams above and on the previous page show the optimum road positions for seeing oncoming traffic when approaching a right-hand (1) and left-hand (3) bend.

ANTICIPATION

Anticipation is the link from what you see to what you think might happen next. It's being one step ahead of a hasty decision.

Anticipation is also the process of guessing what other road users will do next. The expert driver will use this skill in order to plan ahead to maximise progress. However,

making good progress does not have to mean driving at speed.

Anticipating hazards in advance, rather than being forced to stop suddenly, is part of defensive driving, and will result in you maintaining your progress and reaching your destination probably just as soon, more safely, and with less stress all round.

PLANNING

Planning is closely linked to **anticipation;** it involves looking ahead as far as possible and making decisions about how best to proceed.

In addition, planning is linked to **space management.**

It is possible to adapt your driving so that you are **in control over the area around your vehicle.** (The exception to this is, of course, the area directly above you; it is estimated that 0.5% of road accidents happen as a result of objects falling from above, such as heavy objects deliberately thrown from motorway bridges on to vehicles passing below.)

You should aim to drive so as to be surrounded (whenever possible) by a sufficient amount of **space.**

This is especially important when driving on **motorways.**

Here are some examples of times and places where you would use anticipation and planning.

● When there are several lanes to choose from at a roundabout, try to make your choice as early as possible, using the information you receive in advance from road signs and road markings. (To check your knowledge of which lane to choose, see the diagrams on the next page.)

If you cannot see the side mirrors of the long vehicle ahead, the driver is unaware you are there. Keep well back.

Some people find it helps to think of defensive driving as being sur-rounded by a 'bubble' of space.

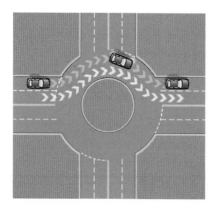

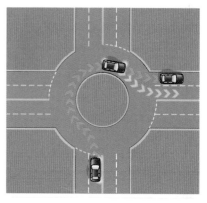

Where there are several road signs displayed on one post, you should read them from the top downwards. The top sign normally relates to the first hazard you will meet.

- When you are following a long vehicle and approaching a roundabout, you should anticipate that the driver may select a different lane from the one a car would use, because of the difficulties of manoeuvring a long vehicle around a tight circle (see diagram below).

- When following a cyclist or horse-rider at a roundabout, anticipate that they may keep to the left and

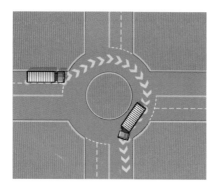

continue around the outside of the roundabout, passing exits which you intend to use.

- As roundabouts become more complex, it is not always easy to make the right choice of lane. You may even have to rely on the information on the tarmac as you go round, especially on a spiral (or helical) roundabout. A good tip is to select the right-hand lane if the exit you want is 'after 12 o'clock' on the sign. Another advantage of choosing the right-hand lane is that if you do make a mistake, and other drivers do not give you room to correct it, you can always go round again.

- On a motorway or dual carriageway, when you see a sign telling you that a lane is closed ahead, move over in good time, and do not accelerate in an attempt to gain an advantage over others.

- Similarly, anticipate the ending of a section of dual carriageway in good time.

- If you see a box junction marked on the road in front, look ahead

and ensure that your exit is clear before moving into the box, unless you want to turn right and are only prevented from doing so by oncoming traffic.

- If you see a sign warning you of a steep gradient, or other hazard such as a ford, be prepared to change to the appropriate gear in good time.

- If you see a low arched bridge ahead, anticipate that there may be high oncoming vehicles in the middle of the road. Observe the bridge height, which may be too low for commercial vehicles.

Be aware of clues that give information of possible hazards, such as the white 'H' on a red ground that denotes a Hospital, and the lights of an ambulance station or fire station.

A cluster of lamp posts often indicates the presence of a roundabout or junction, or an accident 'black spot'.

- If you see flashing amber lights near a school, prepare to slow down, as a crossing warden may step into the road to let children cross.

- Pay special attention to all other signs that warn you of elderly pedestrians, or people walking on the road.

- When driving on a motorway, watch out for lit signs above or beside the carriageway that warn you of accidents or weather conditions, impose temporary speed limits, or give advance notice of lanes closing.

As part of your responsibility to enable other road users to anticipate your actions, ensure that you give all signals accurately and at the right time. For example, on the motorway, give a signal as you reach the first of the three countdown markers before the junction where you intend to leave the motorway.

VISUAL LINKS

Experienced drivers are always looking out for **visual clues** in their driving environment.

Visual clues include the pointers to potential hazards listed earlier in this section (see page 60), such as the ball bouncing across the road, and the rubbish bags stacked at the roadside. Here are some more examples of visual clues and what they tell you:

- You see a stationary vehicle ahead with the bonnet up.

  Can you see the driver? If not, there is a potential hazard, as he or she may suddenly step out into your path. Look for the driver's feet beneath the stationary vehicle.

- You are driving along a country road on a route you have not travelled before.

  How can you tell when there is likely to be a roundabout or junction to negotiate?

- Using your peripheral vision, you notice a large building alongside the road, partially hidden by trees.

  This should alert you to the possibility of drivers turning in or out of the entrance to the building.

By **linking** these visual clues to each other and **selecting** the most important information from them, you will improve your anticipation skills.

PLANNING YOUR DRIVING IN A TOWN OR CITY

Most traffic collisions occur on roads in towns and cities. Using your skills of observation, anticipation and planning, you can minimise the risk of being involved in an accident.

In any town, there are many different things to observe around you. It is vital to

- visually scan ahead, to the sides, and behind you

- assess what you see

- anticipate what others may do next

- plan your best actions to deal with each hazard safely.

For example, as you drive along a reasonably straight main road, you can see at least three separate sets of traffic lights ahead.

Are the lights marking a junction, or a crossing, or some other hazard? (Check your *Highway Code* for the different signs and road markings associated with Pelican, Puffin and Toucan crossings.) By observing any traffic signs, the layout of the signals and the routes taken by other vehicles, your initial assessment should tell you what sort of hazards lie ahead.

Note: do not restrict your observation to the first set of lights. You should be observing all three sets of signals, and anticipating when each light may change to the next phase. This applies even if the lights are 15 to 30 seconds ahead of you.

Your objective is to avoid stopping – something which can be achieved safely at most traffic signals – and instead arrive at the signal at a moderate speed just after the lights have changed to green.

As you are scanning for hazards around and ahead of you, you should start to anticipate when each light may change to the next phase, and plan your driving to arrive when the lights are green. This planning is linked to your observation of all other road users, and the result is achieved by careful control of your speed.

Timing your approach

The timing of traffic lights at a junction is easy to predict. However, if the traffic lights indicate a pedestrian crossing, the probability of the lights changing to red is likely to be related to the number of pedestrians nearby. Remember there is a guaranteed period of green between each red phase of the lights. Look out for a pedestrian moving

If you observe a queue of traffic waiting at a traffic light, you can use it to help time your approach. When the lights change to green, cars move off at intervals of around one second, and heavy vehicles at around two-second intervals.

towards the crossing with out-stretched arm and finger, or a child approaching. (Whether or not they intend crossing, children love to press the button!) The activated crossing lights will change, but not immed-iately if the green light has only just come back on. So it is useful to be aware of the length of time since the lights last changed phase.

Some drivers find that there is a temptation to speed up as they approach the lights, if those lights have been seen to be green for some time. This must always be resisted. You should **never** accelerate as you approach signals that may turn to red. If you have to brake at the last minute, your stopping distance may be longer than you have allowed for, and if a driver on the intersecting road is jumping the lights, you have less time to avoid a serious accident. This is where **planning** is important.

When you have observed that the lights have shown green for some time, **anticipate the lights will change** and **plan to stop** by reducing your speed slightly. Light pressure on your brakes warns drivers behind that you may need to stop. If the lights remain green, you have lost nothing and can continue on your way.

PLANNING YOUR DRIVING ON A MOTORWAY

The speed and volume of the traffic on motorways mean that you need to develop special skills to control your vehicle effectively. Once on the motorway, you are committed; unable to stop or turn round, you have to 'go with the flow' of the heavy traffic, and sometimes deal with lengthy and frustrating tailbacks in the course of your journey.

Weather conditions can make a considerable difference to stress levels when driving on motorways – fog or rain call for constant concentration and all-round hazard awareness, and spray from larger vehicles can make visibility more difficult.

On a motorway you have to make calculations all the time about

● how much space to leave between you and the vehicle ahead

● where you should position your vehicle to ensure you have sufficient stopping distance in an emergency

● what course you would follow to make your escape in the event of an accident just ahead.

When over-taking a long vehicle in the left lane on a three-lane motorway, try to move out into the middle lane while the outside lane is also clear, so that you have an 'escape route' if the long vehicle pulls out in front of you. Avoid getting caught in the 'three across' trap.

'T and T' stands for 'Tyres and Tarmac'. When pulling up in a queue of traffic, make sure you can see the rear tyres of the car in front touching the tarmac; then you know you have left sufficient room, should you need to pull round the vehicle in front of you.

You should always allow plenty of space

● to react to the actions of other road users

● to leave room for others to make mistakes.

Avoid becoming the 'meat in the sandwich' during overtaking. That is, try not to overtake in the middle lane whilst another car is overtaking you in the third lane – a position where you have no room for manoeuvre in case of a sudden accident. This will require sound judgement of speed, plus your skills of observation and planning.

Use of the hard shoulder

If you have to make use of the hard shoulder as an escape route due to a genuine emergency, make sure you observe these guidelines:

● use the hard shoulder as a deceleration lane

● look well ahead to ensure there is no debris in front

● when you come to a stop, pull over as far to the left as possible.

Remember that the hard shoulder is the most dangerous area of the motorway, for drivers and passengers alike.

CONSIDERATION FOR OTHERS

Most drivers have experienced the frustration of trying to make good progress on a motorway when a driver is occupying a lane where they should not be, apparently oblivious to other traffic around them. As an expert driver, make sure you are fully conversant with the rules about lane use on motorways; do not pull out to overtake unless you are sure that traffic in the lane to your left is moving more slowly than you are, and return to your lane as soon as it is safe and convenient to do so.

Of course, even though it is wrong to 'cruise' in the centre or right lanes, you should never try to intimidate another driver or force them out of the way.

STOPPING DISTANCES

Close following of the vehicle in front is a major cause of road accidents. Make sure you are fully conversant with **stopping distances** – check up on them in *The Highway Code,* and remember the Two-Second Rule (see page 123).

It can be difficult to imagine what the correct stopping distance actually looks like. Here are some ideas for visualising the stopping distance on a motorway:

- The stopping distance at 70mph is 96 metres or 315 feet.

- This is about 24 car lengths.

- 24 car lengths is about the size of a football pitch.

Or, you can make use of the marker posts at the side of the motorway.

- The stopping distance at 70mph is 96 metres.

- The marker posts are positioned 100 metres apart.

Remember that other road users have longer stopping distances; for example, motorcycles and long vehicles. Your vehicle, if heavily laden, will also have a longer stopping distance.

And be prepared for a motorcyclist that you are following to be blown off course – perhaps into your path – by a sudden high wind.

Note: it is very important to **allow at least twice as long to stop on a wet road; and in ice or snow, you need to multiply the stopping distance by 10.**

Reaction times

You should also be aware that different people react to traffic hazards at different speeds. An average driver's speed of reaction is from three quarters of a second to one second.

When you relate this to the stopping distance at 70mph (above), it means that you would travel 16 metres (four car lengths) before you reacted to the hazard.

If you are interested in finding out how fast your reactions are, some driving centres have simulation testers that you can try out.

Leave sufficient room to allow for the mistakes of others. After all, if an accident occurs, the fact that it was not your fault is little consolation.

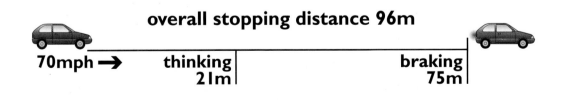

overall stopping distance 96m

70mph ➔   thinking
                 21m

                                    braking
                                    75m

TEST YOUR UNDERSTANDING OF THIS SECTION

1. Why should you try to be proactive when driving?

2. How can road positioning improve your safety when driving?

3. Explain why it is not necessary to drive at high speed to make good progress.

4. How should you proceed if you are not sure which lane to select at a roundabout?

5. At what point should you signal your intention to leave a motorway?

6. Explain the importance of picking up visual clues while driving.

7. Why is it important to plan 'escape routes' when on a motorway?

8. Why should you take extra care when following a long vehicle, or a motorcyclist?

9. Why are reaction times important in relation to stopping distances?

Answers on page 185

Improve your technique

Improve your technique

In this section you will find brief descriptions of a range of **techniques that advanced driving instructors recommend** when you are using:

- the accelerator

- the gears

- the brakes

- the steering

- the lights

- the mirrors

    and hints on

- parking

- overtaking

- dealing with roundabouts, crossings and junctions

- signalling and lane discipline.

You will also find information about driving for economy, observing speed limits, managing distractions, avoiding accidents, and driving at night.

All of these skills are assessed by the AA's instructors when providing Qualified Driver Training courses (see the sample development chart on page 78).

Mental Skills

Improving your practical, manual control skills can add significantly to the enjoyment of driving, both for yourself and for your passengers, and it should also help to make you a safer driver. However, road safety experts place the highest priority on the mental skills used in driving, such as attitude and hazard perception.

Research has shown that the level of vehicle control skills a person has attained at the time of taking their driving test has no connection with how likely they are to be involved in an accident subsequently. After all, a significant number of novice drivers have a collision very soon after passing their test.

Using the controls

THE ACCELERATOR

You should concentrate on accelerating and decelerating **smoothly.** Jerky, uneven acceleration results in an uncomfortable ride for you and your passengers – especially if they are not 'good travellers' – as well as wear and tear on the engine and poor fuel economy.

As you develop sensitivity to your vehicle, you should be able to judge how much pressure on the pedal to apply so that you can keep your progress smooth and your speed constant when going around a **bend:**

● As you approach a bend, assess what would be a safe speed. Slow down to that speed, then select the best gear for mid-revs (see page 80). From the point of where you enter the bend to the point of exit, maintain a constant speed by gentle pressure on the accelerator. This will ensure maximum stability in all conditions.

Try to use this awareness (or 'mechanical sympathy') to **avoid unnecessary braking;** for example, as you approach traffic lights.

Another example is when you are about to enter a 30mph zone. Adjust your speed so that you are travelling no faster than 30mph as you pass the sign (or speed camera!). **Don't wait until you have passed the sign and then brake.**

An instructor's tip: 'Aim to arrive at a green light'; approach the traffic lights at a speed which allows you to stop safely if necessary, or proceed smoothly under full control. (See also pages 70-71.)

Example of a record of development used in the AA's Fleet Driver Training Courses

Driver's name

Instructor's name   Instructor number

Vehicle make   Model   Reg No

Eyesight check *(tick as appropriate)*   PASS ☐   FAIL ☐

	LOW 1	2	3	4	HIGH 5
OBSERVATION					
Use of mirrors	☐	☐	☐	☐	☐
Visual scanning techniques	☐	☐	☐	☐	☐
Observation links	☐	☐	☐	☐	☐
ANTICIPATION					
PLANNING					
Space management	☐	☐	☐	☐	☐
Signalling and communication	☐	☐	☐	☐	☐
Safe use of speed	☐	☐	☐	☐	☐
Safe position on the road	☐	☐	☐	☐	☐
Safety when: Overtaking	☐	☐	☐	☐	☐
Meeting traffic	☐	☐	☐	☐	☐
Crossing traffic	☐	☐	☐	☐	☐
Correct use of vehicle controls	☐	☐	☐	☐	☐
OTHER SKILLS					
Parking and reversing	☐	☐	☐	☐	☐
Concentration and attitude	☐	☐	☐	☐	☐
Security awareness	☐	☐	☐	☐	☐
Fuel efficiency rating	☐	☐	☐	☐	☐

Instructor's comments (identify driver's strengths and weaknesses)

_____

_____

Driver's comments (standard of instruction, personal benefit)

_____

_____

Driver's signature _____

Instructor's signature   Date

Understanding traction

It is useful if you understand the effect that acceleration has on the way the tyres grip the road surface. When the vehicle is accelerating forward **the weight shifts from the front wheels to the back,** thus altering the grip that the front and rear tyres exert relative to each other. So, if you have a front-wheel-drive vehicle, you should be especially careful to avoid harsh acceleration, as this could cause wheel-spin. This is a particular danger in slippery or icy conditions. (See page 83 on 'Cadence braking' for the reverse effect.)

THE GEARS

To get the best out of your vehicle you need to match your acceleration with correct gear changes.

The gears enable you to select the power you need from the engine to perform various tasks.

You will already have learned clutch control as part of your driving test; but you have to re-learn it to some extent every time you drive a new or different vehicle, so that you make smooth progress and avoid jerking the gears. (See 'Driving a new or unfamiliar vehicle', page 134.)

All of the vehicle's controls depend on the way the tyres grip the road surface in order to work effectively. If you would like to know more about this, you can find it explained in greater technical detail in *Roadcraft – The Essential Police Driver's Handbook.*

Some people find it helpful to glance at the rev-counter to know when to change gear. Almost all modern cars, whether petrol or diesel, should be driven between 2,000 and 3,000 revs in most conditions for optimum control and efficiency.

You should make use of 'mechanical sympathy' when changing gear, just as when accelerating:

- assess when you need to change gear by listening to the sound of the engine, or glancing at the rev-counter;

- and get to know at what speed your car is 'ready' to change up or down a gear.

Remember, excessive 'revving' can damage the engine.

THE REV-COUNTER

Your rev-counter can be a useful visual back-up to the information provided by the engine noise – never allow the rev-counter to move into the red.

Characteristics of low and high gears

When in low gear you have plenty of potential **power** (or torque) available to you, but not a great deal of **speed.**

When in a high gear, the opposite is true.

This is why you would select the **highest** gear available to you (fifth on most modern cars) when cruising at a constant speed, for example along a level section of motorway, as this is the best way to make smooth

progress and save fuel (see 'Driving for economy', page 110).

But if you then came to a stretch of the motorway with a **steep gradient,** where lorries were making slow progress, you would need to **change down** a gear in order to supply the torque to overtake them safely.

Here are some other points to bear in mind concerning use of the gears.

- When driving on a **slippery or wet road surface** (in icy conditions, or when there is mud on the road) use the **highest possible gear,** even though you are moving fairly slowly. This is because the high turning power of the lower gears can overcome the grip of the tyres.

- **There is no need to go down through all the gears** when approaching traffic lights, or a road junction. Many years ago learner drivers were taught to do this; possibly because it was thought that the brakes might fail, so it was considered safer to use the gears to slow the car. Instead, you should control the speed by using the brakes, and change to a lower gear when you have reached the required speed; avoid going through all the intermediate gears on the way. Brakes are cheaper to replace than transmission systems.

- **Avoid changing gear when half-way round a bend.** It involves taking one hand off the steering wheel at a time when you need to be in full control, and can adversely affect the stability of the vehicle.

- Don't **rush** your gear changes, or **force** the gear lever if there is any resistance. If you are inclined to rush your gears, try counting '1–2' slowly as you change gear.

- Don't **rest your hand on the gear lever** for longer than necessary – return it to the steering wheel.

- Don't **'coast'** with the clutch down, or the gear lever in neutral.

- If your clutch control is rough when you start the car moving forward, try **slowing down your actions.** Bring the clutch pedal up to biting point and hold it for a few seconds, before easing your foot gently off the pedal.

- Once you have reached the highest gear required, **remove your foot from the clutch** and rest it to the left of the pedal.

Automatic gearboxes

If you have an automatic car, it will do most of the 'thinking' for you where changing gear is concerned, leaving you more time to concentrate on the rest of your driving. You are also able to keep both hands on the wheel. However, there are times when you may need to manually engage a gear; consult your manufacturer's manual to find out when this is recommended.

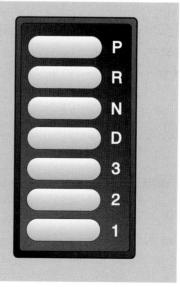

THE BRAKES

Effective use of the brakes relies on the key skill of **anticipation.** Being aware well in advance of the need to slow down or stop enables you to brake smoothly and in a controlled manner.

Experienced drivers are able to **estimate the distance needed for safe braking at different speeds** – again, this relates to developing 'mechanical sympathy' with your vehicle (see above). It also means that you should take note of any alteration in your vehicle's braking capacity, and have any necessary repairs (e.g. worn brake pads – leaking brake fluid check) done promptly.

Testing the brakes should form part of the routine of regular checks you should carry out on your vehicle. And always remember to test the brakes if they become wet – for example, after driving through a flood or ford. For further advice on this, see page 83.

When to apply the brakes

It is possible to slow the vehicle just by easing off the accelerator without applying the brakes; as with moving gently down through the gears, this results in **'engine braking'.**

There are times when this is the best technique to use; for example, on a slippery road where the tyres have less grip.

But in most circumstances you will use the brakes to bring the vehicle to a stop.

You will have learned the correct sequence for stopping normally in order to pass your driving test, but it is possible to get into bad habits later on.

Here is a reminder:

- Check your mirrors, and give a signal to other road users (including cyclists and pedestrians) if necessary

- Ease off the accelerator pedal.

- Press the brake pedal more firmly at first, and then lighten the braking as you approach the stopping point.

- Just before the vehicle stops, depress the clutch pedal fully.

- As the vehicle comes to a stop, release the pressure on the brake slightly, to avoid jolting your passengers (unless you are on a slope).

- Apply the handbrake and put the gear lever in neutral.

Cadence braking

Cadence braking is a technique that can be used by experienced drivers to prevent skidding in wet or icy conditions.

When you brake, the weight of the vehicle is transferred from the back wheels to the front, so that steering becomes more difficult, and the rear tyres do not grip so effectively. If the road surface is slippery, you are likely to go into a skid.

Cadence braking involves applying the brake and then releasing it fully, repeating this pattern so that you can slow down while the brakes are on, and steer the vehicle when they are released.

Note: cars with electronically controlled stability features (or ESP) will avoid skids; the ESP will control the car if its direction on the road is different from the steering input. In severe weather or road conditions, ESP can be very valuable.

ABS

The effect of cadence braking is produced automatically if you have an anti-lock braking system (or ABS). In an emergency, applying and maintaining pressure on the brake pedal will activate the ABS. The ABS will automatically apply and release the brakes in quick succession, thus avoiding the wheels locking and losing grip.

If the tyres' grip on the road surface is lost for other reasons such as skidding or driving on ice, ABS will have no effect at all, and cannot increase traction.

Note: a driver who is employing good observation, anticipation and planning skills avoids the use of ABS.

Braking on bends

As with acceleration (see previous section), it is desirable to avoid braking on bends. This is because:

- braking affects the stability of the vehicle

- it is more difficult to steer while braking.

Brake before you go into the bend, so that you enter the bend at a safe speed and remain in optimum control of the vehicle. Remember:

slow before the bend then keep a constant speed around it.

After a ford

Remember to 'dry out' your brakes after crossing a ford. Use gentle pressure on the brake pedal with your left foot, while gently pressing the accelerator with your right.

If you ever experience ABS, it will feel very 'lumpy', as if you were driving on a bad road surface – there is nothing wrong with the vehicle.

Remember that touching the brake pedal shows the brake lights to following drivers, helping others to anticipate your actions.

THE STEERING

Before you start the car, make sure that your seat is correctly adjusted, so that you are able to hold the steering wheel comfortably in one of the two correct positions:

'ten to two' or **'quarter to three'.**

Note: these two positions are also the most relaxing for your shoulders.

When driving you should not need to be constantly moving the wheel; when you need to steer in any direction, the 'pull-push' method you were taught as a learner driver is the best one to use in nearly all driving situations.

The 'pull-push' method

- Pull the wheel from the top first with one hand, followed by a push from below with the other hand. You should always pull the wheel first in the direction you intend to turn.

- *Do not steer 'hand-over-hand'.* If you cross your hands whilst steering you risk losing control of the vehicle. You would not be able to add a further turn if the corner you were negotiating suddenly turned out to be much sharper than expected, and the vehicle could swing out dangerously towards the opposite side of the

road. (See also 'Airbag safety', page 50.)

- Always keep at least *one* hand on the wheel! This may sound like plain common sense, but many drivers indulge in bad habits such as resting their hand on the wheel and their elbow on the window frame or arm rest, or placing both hands on their lap with only a finger-tip controlling the wheel.

For optimum control, return both hands to the wheel as soon as you can, after removing one in order to change gear, give a signal etc.

Know your vehicle

Again, mechanical sympathy plays a part; get to know how your particular vehicle steers.

Develop a technique for steering smoothly that will save wear and tear on your vehicle and provide an enjoyable ride for you and your passengers. Look up and ahead, and move the wheel slowly and smoothly.

Remember that you may need to re-think this technique each time you drive a new, or different, vehicle. This is especially true if you have been driving a vehicle equipped with **power-assisted steering,** and you then change to one without it (or vice-versa).

Another bad habit is to loosen your grip and allow the wheel to spin back into place by means of its self-correcting mechanism. While this is happening you have no control over the vehicle.

Don't forget that for your vehicle's steering to function properly, the tyres must be inflated to the correct pressures.

Be aware of any **change in the feel of the steering:** for example, if you suddenly hit a patch of surface water, your steering will begin to feel 'light,' letting you know that you have to deal with a hazard.

Steering into skids

The hazard described above is known as **'aquaplaning'.** Driving on ice or slippery road surfaces, when you are at risk of skidding, causes a similar problem.

Skidding is frequently caused by excessive speed for the prevailing conditions, erratic steering, or over-harsh braking, so you should make every effort to avoid these.

If a skid occurs, the first action is to remove its cause.

● If heavy braking locks the wheels and causes a rear-wheel skid, then

first release the brake.

● If harsh acceleration reduces road grip, then stop accelerating.

● If an erratic steering move reduces stability, it will almost always be combined with excessive speed – so reduce your speed.

The vehicle must be allowed to recover its grip on the road surface before steering is effective.

In general, the best technique in the event of a skid is to **steer in the direction of the skid** until the wheels are able to grip the road surface, and then steer in the required direction.

However, road and traffic conditions may render this difficult, and the best advice is to use your skills of hazard perception, anticipation and planning to **minimise the risk of skidding in the first place.**

For experience of controlling a skidding vehicle, try training on a 'skid pan', or in a skid simulator; contact your local Road Safety Officer for information.

TEST YOUR UNDERSTANDING OF THIS SECTION

1. If you failed your practical driving test more than once, are you more likely than the average driver to be involved in an accident for which you were to blame?

2. What effect does acceleration have on the way the tyres grip the road?

3. What is the function of the gears?

4. How should you change gear when approaching traffic lights?

5. Why is it best to avoid braking, or changing gear, on a bend?

6. What is meant by: 1) engine braking, 2) cadence braking?

7. Why is 'hand-over-hand' steering considered bad practice?

8. Why would it be dangerous to allow the steering wheel to return to the central position automatically?

9. What is the basic approach to dealing with a skid?

10. What would you notice when driving a vehicle fitted with power-assisted steering for the first time?

Answers on pages 187–8

Using the lights and mirrors

Your vehicle should have the full complement of front and rear lights, all in working order.

There should be **two main beam** and **two dipped beam headlights.** For each pair, the two lamps should match each other in size and shape, and give out light of a similar intensity.

In most modern cars, sidelights (or **position lights**) consist of a separate bulb within the main headlight fitting, operated by a control on the headlight switch (see also page 88). Position lights should not be used in place of headlights for night driving, but may be used when you want to be sure that the vehicle is seen – for example, in early evening light conditions.

All cars built since 1 January 1971 are required to have at least **two red brake lights** at the rear; and cars

Remember that you need to fit headlight converters before driving your right-hand drive car in countries where they drive on the right instead of the left.

The Highway Code explains the circumstances where you could, theoretically, drive on position lights only, but these are few and far between.

built since 1 April 1980 must have at least **one rear fog lamp.** In addition, **two red reflectors** must be fitted, one on each side. Most cars also have front fog lights; **these should only be switched on when visibility is down to 100m or less, and should be switched off as soon as visibility improves.**

HEADLIGHTS

Get your garage to check that your headlights are adjusted to the correct angle. If the beam is too high, oncoming drivers will be dazzled; if too low, your field of vision will be limited.

You may need to adjust the setting when the rear of your vehicle is heavily loaded (see page 145), but remember to re-adjust to normal later. There may be a 'quick-adjust' control fitted in your vehicle; check in your manual for how to operate this.

The alignment of your headlights will also be checked as part of the car's MOT test.

You must always **use your headlights for night driving.**

Don't drive on **position lights only;** there was a time when drivers switched to sidelights to 'save the

battery' (drivers in the London area would even 'flash' other drivers if they had their dipped headlights on), but this is no longer considered good practice, and you should use your headlights to **see and be seen.**

You should always use dipped headlights **in the daytime too when visibility is poor,** for example in rain or mist. In some countries where visibility is a recurring problem, for example where patchy fog presents a hazard in Canada, the headlights are set to come on when the car is started, as driving with them on has such a positive effect on safety.

When visibility is seriously reduced, **fog lights** are appropriate.

However, there are several points to bear in mind concerning the use of fog lights; in particular, the importance of **switching them off as soon as visibility improves, so that you do not dazzle other drivers.** Fog lights (and other combinations of 'extra' headlights) are regrettably used by some drivers to dazzle and intimidate others. This is a clear demonstration of driver aggression (see pages 23 and 90), and can lead to the other driver becoming temporarily blinded and losing control of their vehicle.

If you find yourself dazzled in this way, slow down or even stop until your vision is back to normal.

In some situations when driving at night you benefit from more warning of road and traffic conditions than you would have in daylight. You can use the headlights of oncoming vehicles to anticipate their approach, and also to assess, for example, the sharpness of a bend ahead.

Here are some more points to consider on the subject of being dazzled by lights.

- **Badly adjusted** headlights can also dazzle other drivers; especially if caught in the mirrors of the car ahead.

- If lights dazzle you from behind – whether badly adjusted headlights, or because the driver is deliberately using their full beam – try **dipping the rear-view mirror.** This deflects the beam from the lights behind to enable you to see. But remember to return it to the normal position shortly afterwards, as it can also distort your judgement of distance with regard to following vehicles.

- Remember to **switch off** front and rear fog lights when visibility improves, as these will dazzle the drivers around you.

- It is easy for your eyes to be **drawn to the lights of an approaching vehicle** as if by a magnet. Try this technique: use both eyes to identify the extent of your own headlight beams, looking slightly above and through the lights of the oncoming traffic.

In order for your lights to work effectively, they must be clean. Use soapy water and a soft cloth to remove dirt and grime. If there is a film of grease coating the lights, it will reduce visibility and increase glare. Also check for stone-holes in the lenses.

One risky aspect of the habit of 'flashing' others to allow them to go first is that in some countries the flashing means just the opposite – 'Give way, I am intending to proceed'.

Flashing headlights at other motorists

Instructors will have different views on whether it is ever permissible to flash your lights at other road users; for example, to give a warning of a hazard ahead.

The Highway Code states that the **only** reason for flashing your lights is **to let others know you are there.**

It is clear that you should certainly not use flashing lights as a means of **intimidating others** or indicating to them to get out of the way.

Many people flash their lights to indicate that they are **letting another motorist go first.** But in general, you should not assume it is safe to proceed on the basis of such a signal – the lights may not be flashed at you, but at someone else.

Using dipped and main beam headlights

Main beam headlights are vital on country roads where there are no street lights. But when driving in the UK, it is unusual to be able to drive for long stretches on main beam, because another vehicle will almost always shortly appear on the road ahead, or approaching from the opposite direction – always dip your lights, but then revert to main beam as soon as possible.

Drivers do not always observe the correct technique for changing from dipped to main beam lights when **overtaking.**

● When you move out to overtake, you should keep your headlights dipped until you are level with the other vehicle, then change to main beam when there are no other vehicles ahead of you or approaching.

HAZARD WARNING LIGHTS

Anyone who aims to be an expert driver will be all too aware of the abuse of hazard warning lights by drivers who use them to park illegally.

Using hazard warning lights while stationary

In general, you should only switch on your hazard warning lights while stationary if your vehicle breaks down and becomes a danger to other traffic. Do not use them for poor or illegal parking.

Using hazard warning lights while driving

You are also allowed to switch your hazard warning lights on for a short period if you are driving on a road subject to a 70 mph speed limit and need to warn following drivers of an obstruction ahead (but not on a road with a lower speed limit). Hazard warning lights should be used only as long as needed to warn following drivers that you are slowing down for a hazard ahead, to avoid a rear-end shunt.

Except in this situation, do not drive with your hazard warning lights switched on. **Do not** use them for towing or being towed.

PARKING LIGHTS

Older drivers may recall the use of small 'parking lights' designed to be suspended out of a car window when 'lighting-up time' regulations were in force. For today's drivers, the terms 'parking lights' and 'sidelights' have been replaced by 'position lights'. When you park at night in a road that is not subject to a speed limit of 30mph or less, you must leave sidelights switched on when you leave the vehicle.

The Highway Code requires that parking lights be displayed when you park on a road (or lay-by) at night where there is a speed limit greater than 30mph. But in built-up areas, you may park without lights provided your vehicle is facing in the correct direction, that is, in the same direction as the traffic flow.

Note: this does not apply to larger vehicles, and those with projecting loads or trailers, which must still display lights.

All mirrors leave you with a blind spot somewhere. You can judge where it is while driving on a motorway, by watching to see how long it takes an over-taking vehicle to draw along-side you, after it has ceased to be visible in your door mirror.

LIGHTS AND YOUR STOPPING DISTANCE

Finally – remember that your stopping distance is dictated by being able to stop **within the distance you can see to be clear.**

When driving at night this will of course change to '**within the distance illuminated by your headlights'.** So you may have to adjust your **speed** accordingly.

USING THE MIRRORS

The mirrors play a key part in enabling you to carry out any manoeuvre in safety.

Note: **convex mirrors** offer a wider field of view, and tend to make other vehicles look further away. **Flat mirrors** give a more restricted field of view but a more accurate impression of distance.

All learner drivers are taught to memorise '**M**SM – **M**irror, **S**ignal, **M**anoeuvre', but experienced drivers can easily get out of the habit of using their mirrors as often as they should.

As part of your routine checks when getting into the car, you should ensure that all mirrors are correctly adjusted for you to see clearly in them.

- If there are several drivers in the family, the rear view mirror may have been left adjusted for someone else, and it would be dangerous to begin driving without realigning it.

  (*Note:* it is a **legal** requirement that you must adjust your mirrors correctly before you start driving.)

- The side mirrors are at risk of being knocked out of position while the vehicle is parked in a busy car park or at the roadside. After starting the engine, always check again that you can see clearly in them.

- If your vehicle stands outside, use a soft cloth to remove any dirt or condensation before starting your journey.

Correct use of the mirrors is vital every time you approach a **roundabout** or **junction,** or prepare to **overtake** or **reverse.**

You use the mirrors to check behind you before **changing lanes,** to assess the amount of approaching traffic and its speed, and to make sure you have sufficient space available. This is especially important on motorways and dual carriageways. Here are some more driving instructors' tips.

When **reversing,** all your mirrors are useful, but you should look mainly through the rear window. (For more on reversing, see page 95).

You can use your left side mirror to **help you judge your position on the road.** Use it to see how far out you are from the kerb, and from drains and markings along the road edge; and when overtaking, take note of whether you are too close to or too far away from the vehicle you're passing; and when moving into the left-hand lane to leave a roundabout.

Use your left-hand mirror to check for **cyclists** before:

- moving off at traffic lights

- moving off in a queue of traffic

- changing lane or position to the left

- turning left

- allowing a passenger to open a door.

(See also page 89 on adjusting your mirror to prevent being dazzled at night.)

When driving on a motorway, you need to start looking in your mirrors far earlier than for other roads, as well as looking much farther ahead. Remember: use your mirrors before you signal and then carry out your overtaking manoeuvre.

TEST YOUR UNDERSTANDING OF THIS SECTION

1. What is the correct way to align your headlights?

2. In what conditions should you use dipped headlights for daytime driving?

3. When should you use fog lights?

4. What can you do to avoid dazzling other drivers with your lights?

5. When, according to *The Highway Code,* is it acceptable to flash your lights at other drivers?

6. While overtaking, should your headlights be on dipped or main beam?

7. In what circumstances should you switch on your hazard warning lights?

8. Why should you always look in your mirrors before changing lanes?

9. How should you deal with the blind spot in your vision?

10. How can using your left mirror help your road positioning?

Answers on pages 189–90

Hints on parking

Parking is now one of the skills that is assessed in the Driving Test, but many experienced drivers still have problems in this area – perhaps because they were never taught the right way to park when they were learning to drive.

Being able to park neatly by reversing into a space between two cars is a useful accomplishment that you can learn with the help of your advanced driving instructor. If you know that you often end up with your back wheels on the kerb and the

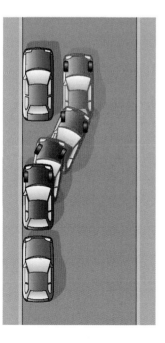

front of your vehicle sticking out into the road, why not take steps to learn how to park correctly?

Reversing makes the best use of the car's manoeuvrability. It is always ideal to reverse into any parking space, including driveways. Simply, you are putting the back of your car into a **limited space** where visibility is most difficult, but where you can maintain good observation to ensure the safety of yourself and others. When driving away from the parking space, you have optimum forward observation ability, as you move into an area used by other cars and pedestrians.

When preparing to reverse into a parking bay that is either square to the traffic flow or angled in a herring-bone pattern, take as much space forward as you can. Drive slowly past the space, looking into it as you pass (is it long enough and wide enough for your needs?). Then, as the rear of the vehicle is in line with the space, steer briskly away from it, to line up the rear of the vehicle, ready to enter the space. Continue to move forwards very slowly, and straighten the steering so

If parking on a steep gradient, it may be wise to leave the vehicle with first gear engaged, and with the steering wheel turned towards the kerb.

If the two vehicles are the same size, you can line up the two steering wheels.

Your vehicle will not fit into a space less than 1½ times its length. Don't even try it!

that when you reverse, the car is aimed at the space and very little steering adjustment should be needed.

When parking parallel to the kerb at the roadside, the sequence you should aim for is as follows:

- Look for a space one-and-a-half times the length of your car (or start with twice the length and work down, if you prefer).

- Check in your mirrors for following traffic, and indicate if necessary. Don't forget to look over your right shoulder and stop if necessary while carrying out the manoeuvre.

- Position your vehicle so that it is parallel with and forward of the leading edge of the vehicle you are parking behind. Reverse back until your rear bumper is in line with its rear bumper. You should be about two or three feet away from the other vehicle.

- Check again over your right shoulder, then begin to reverse slowly, at the same time turning the steering wheel briskly to the left. You should aim the offside rear corner of your car at the nearside front corner of the car behind. (If you are parking

between two vehicles, take care also to clear the rear corner of the vehicle in front.)

- Next, turn the wheel briskly to the right and continue reversing until your wheels are lined up parallel to the kerb.

- Straighten up and move forward a little if necessary.

This manoeuvre is easier if you have a vehicle with power-assisted steering, but care and practice will result in a clear improvement, whatever vehicle you drive.

If you are unsure about where you may and may not park, check *The Highway Code* for a comprehensive list of restricted places.

Don't forget to check that you have left other drivers adequate room to proceed past you or get out after you have parked your vehicle. And don't forget to switch off the lights and engine before you leave the vehicle. Make sure the handbrake is on. If parking on a gradient, leave the car in first gear (or 'park' on an automatic car), with the wheels turned towards the kerb.

Finally, remember to lock your vehicle.

Overtaking

When overtaking, there are three questions you should always ask yourself:

- **Is it safe?**

- **Is it legal?**

- **Is it necessary?**

In today's crowded traffic conditions, **opportunities for overtaking are limited.** There is little point in adopting an attitude where you are constantly putting pressure on yourself and others through trying to make faster progress, if your efforts result only in your moving a little farther up a slow-moving line of traffic.

You may be able to use your **local knowledge** to anticipate whether, for example, there is a stretch of dual carriageway ahead where you will be able to overtake more safely; or you may know that the slow-moving vehicle that is holding you up normally turns off at a particular point.

But you can never be sure that this will happen, so do not take risks.

When you need to overtake, you should **position your vehicle** so that you can see clearly ahead, and assess whether you have adequate space to complete the manoeuvre in safety.

When overtaking *you should not:*

- drive too close to the vehicle in front

- accelerate too quickly or harshly

- follow the vehicle in front into overtaking when you yourself cannot see clearly ahead

- overtake a vehicle that is indicating right, even if you think the indicator has been left on in error

- overtake on the left, unless the vehicle in front is signalling to turn right and you have room to do so, or where traffic in a motorway lane is temporarily moving more slowly than the traffic in the lane to the right. You can also pass on the left when in a one-way street, and when you are in a dedicated left-turn lane.

Never overtake on a bend, on the brow of a hill, or when approaching a humpback bridge.

Many experienced drivers are surprisingly unfamiliar with the true dimensions of their vehicle, and swing out much wider than they need to overtake, as well as assuming they cannot get through the space next to a vehicle that is waiting to turn. Get to know the size of your vehicle, so that you can manoeuvre in safety and with confidence.

It is very bad practice to be **forced to cut short an overtaking manoeuvre half-way through** because you have not assessed the available space correctly. This is something you should particularly bear in mind when overtaking **long vehicles.**

You should **never overtake when there is a junction ahead.** For example, if you were to overtake just before a side road that joins from the left, a car emerging from the side road could collide with your vehicle as you move in to return to the left side of the road. In the same way, you should take extra care when overtaking near a driveway or entrance to a pub, petrol station or supermarket.

Be observant and obey all road signs and markings in areas where overtaking is forbidden, such as the approaches to pedestrian crossings and level crossings. Check the list of these places in *The Highway Code.*

LEFT-HAND-DRIVE VEHICLES

When overtaking a left-hand-drive vehicle, bear in mind that the blind spot on that vehicle is much greater than on a right-hand drive vehicle. Avoid holding a position in the area where you are unable to see the driver in their mirrors, and *'pass the vehicle positively and promptly'.*

TEST YOUR UNDERSTANDING OF THIS SECTION

1. What size of space should you select (if possible) when reverse-parking between two vehicles?

2. How should you position your vehicle when preparing to park in reverse?

3. In which direction should you first turn the steering wheel when carrying out reverse parking?

4. List some places where you are not allowed to park.

5. What questions should you ask yourself before overtaking?

6. How can local knowledge assist you in deciding whether you need to overtake?

7. List some situations where you should not overtake.

8. Why must you take special care when overtaking a long vehicle?

Answers on page 190–91

Dealing with roundabouts and junctions

Any place where traffic joins or merges represents a hazardous driving situation.

Most accidents occur because two or more vehicles are attempting to occupy the same space at the same time (see 'High-risk driving situations', page 41).

JUNCTIONS

When approaching a junction, always move into the appropriate position on the road in good time, so that other road users know what you intend to do.

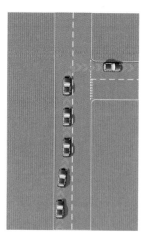

The correct positions for turning right or left are indicated in the diagrams below; avoid swinging out wide in order to turn left (only long vehicles are allowed to do this), and leave room if possible for following traffic to pass on the left if you are waiting to turn right.

At a marked crossroads, two options are available when vehicles approaching from opposite directions both intend to turn right (see diagram on next page). The preferred route is to pass right side to right side; however, passing left side to left side generally gives a clearer view. Passing right side to right side is sometimes compulsory, due to road markings, or more appropriate for the road layout.

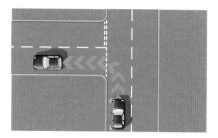

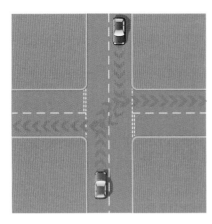

Cyclists and motorcyclists

Look out for cyclists and motorcyclists when you approach a junction.

When turning left, use your rear view and left door mirrors to check that you are not going to trap a cyclist when you turn.

You also need to look out for cyclists when you are emerging from a junction.

Pedestrians

It is very important, when you are turning into a side road, to remember that **any pedestrians who have begun to cross the road have priority.** Adjust your speed sufficiently before turning so that you have full control, and could stop if necessary.

Junctions with STOP signs and GIVE WAY signs

Experienced drivers sometimes seem to forget that

at a STOP sign – you must stop!

Wait at the solid white line until it is safe to proceed.

A 'Give Way' sign is sometimes preceded by a triangle marked on the road.

Wait at the broken white line and **give way** to traffic on the major road.

Some junctions have **advanced stop lines,** where buses or cyclists can wait ahead of other traffic. See *The Highway Code* if you are not sure what these look like, and watch out for them when driving.

Remember an instructor's tip about thinking of the round-about as a clock-face; if your destina-tion is 'after 12 o'clock', select the right lane. And if you are unable to exit when you wish due to traffic volume, then simply go round again.

ROUNDABOUTS

When you approach a roundabout:

- Look early to assess the speed and density of traffic already on the roundabout, so that you can vary your approach speed to join the flow safely.

- The basic rule is 'Give way to traffic already on the roundabout, usually from the right' – but do not get into the habit of **looking to the right and turning left;** you could easily collide with a vehicle ahead of you. It is vital to look all round for traffic as you move on to the roundabout. Look at least twice in every direction.

- Remember that you cannot assume that others will take up the correct position for their intended exit from the roundabout – or even signal their intention to leave it in the correct manner.

For more tips on roundabouts, check the relevant sections in *The Highway Code.*

MINI-ROUNDABOUTS

Mini-roundabouts are installed in many places where there is insufficient room to site a 'proper' roundabout, so there is often little room to negotiate them.

The question then arises – *are you allowed to drive over rather than round them?*

You may be surprised to find that *The Highway Code* makes it clear that you **MUST** drive **around** the mini-roundabout where there is room to do so, and where your vehicle is small enough. In *The Highway Code,* the word 'MUST' is printed in capitals and in red; this means that it relates to a law (under the Road Traffic Act or other legislation).

So you should make every effort to treat a mini-roundabout as you would any other roundabout.

When you encounter a cluster of mini-roundabouts (or 'magic roundabouts'), you need to use even more care and concentration, as these can be confusing, and **clear signalling** is important.

Signalling on roundabouts

Here is a reminder of the conventions for signalling at roundabouts.

- If leaving at the first exit:

   keep in the left lane and signal left as you approach the roundabout.

- If going straight ahead:

   keep in the left lane unless road markings tell you to do otherwise. Indicate left once you have passed the exit before the one you're taking.

- If going more than half-way round:

   indicate right and select the right-hand lane, but use your mirrors and indicate left in good time before leaving the roundabout.

For more about Signalling, see the following section.

On complex roundabouts, sometimes vehicles on a major route have priority because the road passes through the roundabout. The best advice is to look every-where to gain the maximum information from all signs and road mark-ings, and make an early deci-sion. Don't try to change lanes at the last moment. See also diagram, page 66.

TEST YOUR UNDERSTANDING
OF THIS SECTION

1. Why should you take extra care at roundabouts and junctions?

2. What kind of road users should you particularly look out for when turning left into a side road?

3. What is the purpose of advanced stop lines?

4. Describe the best way to move into the stream of traffic on a roundabout.

5. How should you proceed when you encounter a cluster of mini-roundabouts?

6. If you are not sure which exit you need from a roundabout, which lane should you select initially?

Answers on page 192

Signalling and lane discipline

SIGNALLING

It's important to remember that the purpose of signals is to provide **information** to other road users – rather than to give them **orders!**

Signalling too late, or not at all, is one of the bad habits that people can easily get into after they have been driving for some time.

Note: don't forget that signalling *too far in advance* can cause problems too – for example, when intending to turn off into a minor road.

INDICATOR SIGNALS

There are many different kinds of signals that can be given by motorists, but generally you signal your intention to change direction, overtake etc, by means of your **indicators.** Generally, you should allow enough time to check your mirrors and give four flashes of the indicator **before** commencing the change of road position.

You should indicate whenever it is necessary to let oncoming and following traffic know what you intend to do; but *if there is no other traffic,* a signal is not always needed (but remember other road users, such as pedestrians, who may need to know your intentions).

It is also not necessary to indicate every time you pull out to pass a parked car, especially if the whole length of the road you are driving along is lined with parked cars.

And when moving off from a stationary position, use your indicator only if traffic is approaching from either direction.

On the other hand, you will of course use your indicators frequently when driving on motorways, and when changing lanes or overtaking on other roads.

Avoid cancelling your indicator too early while carrying out a manoeuvre; this could cause other road users to think you have changed your mind.

BRAKE LIGHTS AND REVERSING LIGHTS

Brake lights and reversing lights are another form of giving signals, since they automatically convey the information that you are slowing down and perhaps intend to stop, or that you intend to reverse your vehicle.

THE HORN

The horn is an audible warning device, and is not used very frequently (at least in the UK) – indeed many drivers only use their horn when they want to signal anger and frustration!

The Highway Code states that the only reason for using the horn is **to alert other road users to your presence.**

Occasions when it could be appropriate to sound your horn include:

- while waiting to proceed at a dangerous crossroads where visibility is very limited

- when another driver is waiting to emerge onto your road and appears to be looking away from you, and you feel they have not seen you coming.

OTHER KINDS OF SIGNALS

References to **hand or arm signals** are still found in the Theory Test, but it is very rare for drivers to use them today; however, it is useful to know what they are, as they can be helpful to reinforce an indicator's signal – for example, at a zebra crossing. Illustrations of arm signals are found in the last section of *The Highway Code*.

It is good manners to acknowledge courtesy from other drivers, but only when you can do so safely; if it would be dangerous to take your hand away from the wheel to wave your thanks, a smile will fit the bill. (Any other hand signals used by drivers are probably inappropriate ones!)

Where a courtesy wave is to be given, use the left hand near the centre of the windscreen, or, for the benefit of a following driver, just below the mirror.

Remember that you should never wave pedestrians across at crossings (see page 43) – there is always the risk that another driver will break the law by overtaking while you are waiting at the crossing, so it is best to let the pedestrian be responsible for their own safety.

If you are coming up to **traffic lights with lanes**, look ahead and note whether the lanes merge beyond the lights; this will aid your choice of lane.

107

You may sometimes have to cross a bus, cycle or tram lane in order to turn off the road. Look carefully all round, and give way to buses, cycles or trams.

LANE DISCIPLINE

Lanes are found on all but the smallest roads, and being able to make good use of them is a sign of an experienced driver.

The ideal technique is to **look ahead as far as possible,** so that you can judge which choice of lane will enable you to make the best progress. For example, if the right-hand lane can be used either by traffic turning right or traffic going straight ahead, and you can see that it is mainly occupied by traffic waiting to turn right, then your best choice for proceeding straight ahead is to use the left-hand lane.

Despite your best efforts, you will sometimes end up in the wrong lane – perhaps at a filter where 'right lane must turn right'. Unless traffic is very light and you have the opportunity to move to the correct lane, you should continue in your present lane, and turn round when there is an opportunity to do so safely; or you could drive round the one-way system if you are in a town centre.

If you intend to turn right at a second junction, where two junctions are close together, move into the right lane as you approach the first junction.

Take care that you do not move into any lane that is reserved for **buses, trams, taxis** or **cycles.**

When on a motorway, take note of road signs and lights next to or above the carriageway warning you of **lane closures** ahead, and act on them in plenty of time by signalling and moving into the lanes that are available.

TEST YOUR UNDERSTANDING
OF THIS SECTION

1. What information can you give to other road users by means of your indicators?

2. When would it be safe not to give a signal?

3. When should you sound your horn?

4. Why is it important to select the correct lane at traffic lights?

5. In what lanes must you not drive?

Answers on page 193

Driving for economy

One part of driving for economy has to do with your choice of car, and the other part with how you choose to drive it.

Modern cars are designed with environmental considerations and improved economy continually in mind. The smaller and lighter the car, the less fuel it is likely to need.

For town driving with frequent stops and starts it will make more sense to choose a vehicle of fairly modest size, but if you drive long distances on business, cruising at high speeds for considerable periods, then a car with a larger engine may be more appropriate, and not necessarily less economical. A car with manual gears is likely to be more fuel-efficient than an automatic.

You can save fuel (and do less damage to the environment) by observing the following advice:

- Don't use the car if you don't need to. For short journeys, walk or cycle instead, and use public transport when you can.

- Have your car serviced regularly, and carry out all necessary repairs.

- Know the correct tyre pressures for your vehicle and check them regularly.

- Don't overload your vehicle with luggage and passengers – if you need more space for a particular journey, consider hiring a larger vehicle for the occasion.

- If you decide you need a roof-rack, choose one with an aerodynamic design.

- Do not drive with an empty roof-rack on your car. By increasing drag, the roof rack can eat up more than 10% of your total fuel consumption. Remove the roof-rack when you arrive at your holiday destination, and only re-fit it when it's time to drive home.

- If your vehicle is fitted with air-conditioning, use it sparingly. Air-conditioning increases fuel consumption by more than six per cent for small cars, and by almost 5% for a medium-sized car. However, the additional turbulence and drag caused by driving with a window open at motorway speeds can add 14% fuel consumption per window.

- Provided your vehicle has good ventilation, keep the windows closed, as opening them increases turbulence and makes the vehicle less aerodynamic. Don't forget to close the sun-roof also, when you don't need it open. An open window or sun-roof can account for 7% of fuel consumption for a small car.

- Maintain steady progress and observe speed limits.

- Avoid excessive acceleration followed by harsh braking (for example, when negotiating speed humps). This results in stress on driver and vehicle alike, and uses more fuel than maintaining a constant speed.

(See 'Anticipation', page 64, and 'Space management', page 70.)

- Use the gears correctly (see page 79). Staying in a high gear for too long (for example, when driving uphill) causes the engine

Every time you brake you waste fuel, so coming off the accelerator earlier instead will help.

to labour, and can be wasteful
of fuel.

BUT –

- Remember that you should not
'coast' as a way of saving fuel, as
this is potentially very dangerous
– if the engine should stall, you
will lose power assistance to the
brakes and the steering.

- Using a pulsing action on the
accelerator can lead to heavy fuel
consumption. Use your toes on
the pedals rather than the ball of
your foot.

- Remember when choosing a new
car: the less it pollutes, the less
you pay. New cars registered
from 1 March 2001 attract
vehicle tax benefits if they are
'environmentally friendly'.

TEST YOUR UNDERSTANDING
OF THIS SECTION

1. Why might a vehicle with a
    relatively small engine be a good
    choice for urban driving?

2. How can keeping your car
    windows closed help with fuel
    economy?

3. How can you prevent high fuel
    consumption when you are
    driving on a busy road where
    you have to negotiate frequent
    obstructions?

4. Why should you not use
    'coasting' as a way of saving fuel?

Answers on page 194

Observing speed limits

It is quite possible to agree in principle with the message of a road safety campaign without accepting that the message applies to you.

At the beginning of this book you will find several references to the importance of observing speed limits.

A major cause of road accidents is **inappropriate speed,** and many people do not seem to see breaking the speed limit as a serious offence. Some people exceed the speed limit in their haste to get to an appointment on time; others do so simply because they enjoy the thrill of driving at high speed.

Psychology researchers at the University of Reading have found that many people believe that they are quite safe to drive at high speeds because they are better than the average driver. This is borne out by the fact that people will often tolerate higher speeds when they are driving but not when someone else is driving. In addition, people who claim to be concerned about the risk of having an accident in fact drive at about the same speed as those who profess to be fairly unconcerned!

DO SPEED LIMITS WORK?

It has been proved that whenever existing speed limits are amended, or new ones introduced, there is always **a fall in accident rates.** So there is no doubt that observing the speed limit increases safety for you and for others.

On the other hand, there is no doubt that speed limits cause frustration, and it can be difficult to see the need to observe them on an empty road. So a balance has to be struck which takes account of individual freedom but also guarantees safety for all.

The Government has addressed this problem by considering several ideas for making the situation seem more equitable and acceptable to drivers.

These include:

- Making greater use of **short-term disqualifications,** even for periods as short as a fortnight or a month.

- Reviewing the system of **penalty points,** so as to give the courts more flexibility in awarding the number of penalty points according to the seriousness of the offence. More points could be given for second offences, so as to target the increased threat of disqualification at the worst drivers.

- Introducing more **speed cameras,** since these are known to make drivers slow down – especially if they have been 'caught' before and don't want to add to their total of points, even though they are aware there is a good chance that the camera will not be active.

Where drivers and police share the view that the speed limit is designed to maximise safety, rather than to entrap motorists out of perversity or a need to increase revenue, then the speed limit is doing its job effectively.

In the UK, car crashes are responsible for more deaths of people under 40 than any other factor.

Remember that where there are street lamps spaced less than 185m apart, a 30mph limit applies unless signs on the posts state otherwise.

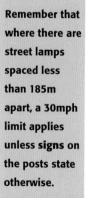

TEST YOUR UNDERSTANDING OF THIS SECTION

1. Why is inappropriate speed a major cause of accidents?

2. How do we know that speed limits are an effective means of reducing accidents?

3. What are the speed limits for different kinds of roads and vehicles, as defined by *The Highway Code?*

4. Why might it be useful for the courts to have a wider range of penalties for exceeding speed limits available to them?

Answers on page 195

Managing distractions

How safe and successful a driver you are does not just depend on technical skills. The way you interact with the environment of the vehicle (both internal and external) is also very important.

All drivers must develop **strategies for managing distractions.** Your attention can be diverted by passengers and devices inside the vehicle, such as

- children

- pets

- car radios

- mobile phones

- route guidance systems.

Experienced drivers rely on the fact that many actions and responses become **automatic** over time, enabling you to converse or listen to the radio while in the car, as you are not having to think about every single move. Examples of these automatic processes include changing gear, using the pedals in combination with each other, and carrying out the 'Mirror Signal Manoeuvre' routine. However, excessive reliance on automatic skills can be risky when road or traffic conditions call for something out of the ordinary.

MAKING CONVERSATION

It might seem reasonable to assume that experienced drivers cope much better than novice drivers with the requirement to do two things (or more) at once; for example, maintaining a conversation while negotiating obstacles in heavy traffic.

After all, the familiar image of the business driver is of someone driving and talking on a mobile phone, while surrounded by other paraphernalia such as a laptop computer and road atlas open on the passenger seat.

In a survey by the AA's Road Safety Unit, 20% of parents admit they have turned round in the driving seat while driving in order to admonish children.

117

The Highway Code advises you **not** to use your mobile phone if you are involved in a motorway accident. Instead, use the (free) emergency phone, which connects you directly to the police and enables them to identify your exact location.

However, research has shown that a driver's **ability to spot hazards is dramatically reduced when they are talking as well as driving;** and that they **take more risks,** such as driving too close to the car in front, and pulling out into too-small gaps in the traffic.

And if the conversation with the passenger takes the form of an argument (perhaps about the other person's map-reading skills), then the aggression generated will have a negative effect on the attitude of the driver, further increasing the risk of accidents.

If **children** are among the passengers, then the driver has to decide exactly how much noise and movement he or she can tolerate, and make this clear to the children before starting the journey. (*Note:* children should be strapped in securely, see page 146.)

For a long journey, it may be best to provide games and activities for the children: get them to count how many of a particular type of building they see, or how many of a particular kind of vehicle. If you prefer minimal noise, provide them with portable cassette or CD players.

MOBILE PHONES

If you are having a conversation on a mobile phone, then the effect on your concentration will be just as great as if you were talking to a passenger.

A hands-free phone is no safer to use than a hand-held one. Even though you can keep both hands on the wheel, your mind is occupied elsewhere.

Mobile phones can be a blessing to motorists, especially in the event of breakdown in a remote place, or any situation where you feel vulnerable; but their use should be restricted to when you are stationary.

To avoid being distracted by incoming calls, turn off the phone while driving, or make use of the message facility so that you can return the call when you have found a safe place to park or pull off the road.

Drivers between the ages of 17–25 are thought to listen to music about 70% of their driving time.

MUSIC WHILE YOU DRIVE

Some people cannot cope with listening to music while driving; others cannot cope without it.

Music can distract you from concentrating on your driving, especially in busy traffic conditions, and can block out the sounds that warn you of approaching hazards (see page 61).

Extremely loud music emanating from a car with its windows open is annoying to pedestrians, and is also likely to have an effect on the attitude of the driver. If you can hear loud music from a nearby car in busy traffic, treat the vehicle with caution: the loud noise means that the driver is at greater risk of collision, and it could be you who becomes involved.

On the other hand, if you are driving at night and feeling tired, or on a long monotonous stretch of motorway where boredom could put you at greater risk of accidents, then upbeat music may help to keep you awake and focused (see page 130).

ROUTE GUIDANCE SYSTEMS

The AA has carried out research into what kinds of guidance systems are the safest, and the least likely to cause distraction to drivers.

You will normally make use of some kind of navigation aids on any journey except a routine one; these include maps, written routes, or looking at direction signs. Listening to traffic information transmitted through the radio is likely to be less distracting than the other methods, all of which involve looking away from the road.

Road junctions are a prime location for accidents, so any guidance system that results in your making confident progress, rather than hesitating at junctions, must be a positive development.

For more about in-car navigation systems, see page 156.

EXTERNAL DISTRACTIONS

The possibilities here are endless, and include the phenomenon known as 'rubber-necking' in the vicinity of an accident.

This is when drivers slow down to look at the accident scene; it seems that the flashing lights of ambulances and other emergency vehicles draw people's gaze like a magnet. Not only is 'rubber-necking' a ghoulish habit, it leads to the forming of queues – especially on a motorway, where every vehicle that slows even by one mile an hour adds to the rapid immobilisation of traffic.

Of course, if you are able to help at an accident scene and can stop in a safe place you should do so (see page 163), but at all other times you should concentrate on the road and avoid being distracted for any reason.

TEST YOUR UNDERSTANDING OF THIS SECTION

1. The ability developed by experienced drivers to carry out some actions automatically can sometimes put them at risk. Why is this?

2. What effect does conversation have on a driver's hazard perception skills?

3. Is it safe to use a hands-free mobile phone while driving?

4. Why should you never indulge in 'rubber-necking'?

Answers on page 196

Avoiding accidents

Remember that in the event of a collision, the rear vehicle is almost always considered to be the one at fault.

Manage the space you occupy, and the space you plan to need, to keep you safe.

The previous section drew your attention to one aspect of driver behaviour that can lead to accidents – **inappropriate speed.**

Another is **'tailgating'**, or **following too closely** behind a vehicle in front of you, and failing to maintain an **appropriate separation distance.**

Tailgating can be dangerous for many reasons. Here are some of them:

- If you are following too closely and the vehicle in front is forced to stop suddenly, you will probably collide with it.

- Even if you do not hit the other vehicle, you need room to manoeuvre if it has broken down.

- Following another vehicle too closely may mean there is insufficient room for an emergency vehicle to get through.

- Tailgating in queuing traffic can result in access to side roads being blocked. Never ignore road markings telling you to keep an area clear.

- Following a long vehicle too closely affects your view of the road ahead, so that you cannot plan your next move effectively or safely.

(See 'Overtaking', page 124.)

- Many drivers tailgate in fog, because the rear lights ahead give them a sense of security. In fact, you should leave a much greater separation distance from the vehicle in front in any kind of adverse weather (see below).

- Tailgating is frequently used by aggressive drivers as a method of harassing and intimidating others – often in combination with flashing headlights (see page 23).

If you are being tailgated, gradually slow down to increase the gap between your vehicle and the one in front, allowing at least double the distance of the two-second rule. If you need to brake, allow for the following driver by braking early and gently, keeping an eye on your mirror. This is called **'braking for two'** – that is, for yourself and the tailgater, ensuring that if you are hit from behind, you will not be shunted into the car ahead of you.

STOPPING DISTANCES AND SEPARATION DISTANCES

While learning to drive, you became familiar with the **stopping distances** that are considered safe for various speeds.

To check on these, look up the chart in *The Highway Code*, which is divided into 'Thinking distance' and 'Braking distance'. Adding the two together gives the **overall stopping distance** (see also page 72).

You can judge distances when driving at low speeds by calculating one yard or one metre per second for each mph of your speed. A simpler method is the two-second rule.

The two-second rule

Driving instructors generally recommend using the 'two-second rule' in preference to the charts in the *Highway Code*, as it is easier to visualise.

You should keep a *minimum* of **two seconds** of travelling distance between your vehicle and the one in front. To measure this, pick a fixed marker on the roadside ahead, such as a signpost. As the vehicle in front passes this marker, start saying aloud 'Only a fool breaks the two-second rule' – a phrase which takes about two seconds to say. If you pass the marker before you have finished saying it, then pull back – you are too close.

You should allow a minimum of **four seconds** in wet weather, and at least **twenty seconds** in icy conditions. This is because your tyres have less grip on the road – see pages 73 and 83.

You should also allow a greater separation distance in fog (see above).

Limitations of the two-second rule

The two-second rule works most effectively in traffic that is flowing freely at speeds above 10mph. It is more difficult to apply when you are travelling at very low speeds. You have to rely on experience to guide you on what is a safe distance for the conditions.

At very high speeds you may feel more comfortable with a longer minimum, such as three or four seconds.

Remember that large vehicles and motorcycles have greater stopping distances than cars.

To assess your separation distance at high speed on a motorway, refer to the recommendations in the chart and use the small numbered posts along the edge of the carriageway, which are exactly 100m apart.

It can be helpful to select a lower gear to enable you to make better progress. This technique would be useful when pulling out to overtake, for example, a slow-moving vehicle such as a tractor or milk float on a hill.

OVERTAKING

Opportunities for overtaking in today's traffic conditions are very limited.

Some drivers wrongly believe that the best technique is to position their vehicle as close as possible to the one they wish to overtake, and then accelerate sharply as soon as they see an opportunity.

This is a dangerous habit to develop, because **visibility is not sufficient to guarantee safety** – especially when overtaking a long vehicle. For example, if you were to pull out and draw level with the other vehicle, only to find you had not enough space to complete the manoeuvre due to approaching traffic, you could end up stranded in the middle of the road if the vehicle behind you has moved up to occupy the space.

The correct method is to position your vehicle two seconds behind the vehicle you are overtaking, and slightly closer to the centre of the road than normal to improve your view of the road ahead. Make sure you have enough engine power at your disposal – usually by choosing one gear lower than that you have been travelling in – select a gear so that the engine is at mid-revs (about 2,000 revs below the red line in either a petrol or diesel engine). Then use your 'MSM' routine, move out confidently when it is safe to do so, pass the other vehicle, and return to your normal position as soon as possible.

Points to remember when overtaking

- Take care that you do not force approaching drivers to slow down or cut in sharply after overtaking.

- Remember not to overtake in the vicinity of a side turning (see page 98).

- Do not follow another vehicle into overtaking if you cannot see clearly ahead yourself.

- Assess your own speed as you close behind the vehicle you intend to overtake – could you still stop safely in an emergency? And assess the speed of vehicles approaching on the opposite carriageway.

- Give motorcycles, horses and cyclists plenty of room when overtaking, and drive slowly, avoiding excessive engine noise.

- If you have to pass stationary vehicles, remember that vehicles on the other side of the road have priority if the obstruction is on your side.

- When overtaking long vehicles, drop back further than you would for a car to increase your visibility before beginning the manoeuvre.

OVERTAKING ON MOTORWAYS

When driving on motorways it is necessary to use your mirrors earlier and look further ahead than on other roads, because of the high speed of the traffic.

- Overtake on the right only, and make sure there is a clear space in the lane you are moving into.

- Don't forget to check your blind spot.

- Remember that traffic may be coming up behind you very quickly; even though the speed limit is 70 mph on all motorways, many drivers regularly exceed this.

In conclusion: when preparing to overtake, you should always ask yourself three questions –

- **is it safe?**

- **is it legal?**

- **is it necessary?**

When overtaking a long vehicle that is travelling on the inside lane, try to have the outside lane clear as well for good measure. Don't get caught as the 'meat in the sandwich'.

TEST YOUR UNDERSTANDING
OF THIS SECTION

1. Why is tailgating dangerous?

2. When would you need to allow more than a two-second gap between your vehicle and the one in front?

3. Where on the road should you position your vehicle when intending to overtake?

4. Give some examples of situations where you should not overtake.

5. Why might you select a lower gear for overtaking?

6. What are the three questions you should ask yourself when deciding whether to overtake?

Answers on page 197

Driving at night and dealing with tiredness

When asked whether they like driving at night, some motorists will reply that they prefer it, and others that they try to avoid it as much as possible.

People who like night driving do so because:

- the roads tend to be **quieter**

- you can pick up **visual clues** earlier, such as the beam of headlights that can warn you of approaching traffic even when the vehicle is still concealed by a bend.

Others find night driving difficult because:

- your **field of vision** is usually more **limited**

- it can be more **difficult to judge distances**

- there is a **risk of being dazzled** by the headlights of other vehicles, if they are badly adjusted or deliberately too bright (see page 89).

Here are some **suggested techniques for maximising safety** for yourself and other road users when you are driving at night.

- Do not allow tiredness to prevent you from checking that your headlights, brake and rear lights are all working *before* you set out on a night-time journey.

- Make sure, too, that headlights are free of dirt and grease, which would make the beam less bright; and that your windscreen is clear of greasy smudges, which affect visibility at night even more seriously than in the day. Wiper blades should be replaced at least once per year, or you will find a murky arc obscuring your vision.

- Adjust your speed, to allow for the fact that you will not be able to see hazards such as stationary vehicles so far ahead as you would in daylight. Remember that tiredness can also affect your vision. (See 'Dealing with tiredness', page 128.)

If headlights from a vehicle behind dazzle you, remember that you can dip your rear view mirror to avert the glare. But return it to the normal position once the glare has gone, because a 'dipped' mirror can make the following vehicle look further away than it really is.

Driver sleepiness is thought to cause at least 10% of all road accidents and one in five of accidents on motorways and major roads.

Frequent light snacks are better than a heavy meal – and especially at lunchtime. And of course, don't have any alcohol before driving.

- Be aware of the increased risk of driving 'on autopilot' at night, when you are tired and there are fewer vehicles on the roads. (See 'Dealing with tiredness', below.)

- Be extra-vigilant about looking out for pedestrians in the dark. They may well not be wearing light-coloured clothing or reflective armbands as recommended in *The Highway Code,* and they may behave in an erratic or unexpected manner; for example, adults coming out of a pub and not looking where they are going, or children walking home after school in the winter months.

Note: a great proportion of pedestrian casualties are **children;** they do not develop the ability to judge the speed of approaching traffic until at least the age of eight, and must always be regarded as 'vulnerable road users'.

DEALING WITH TIREDNESS

One of the major causes of road accidents is drivers who fall asleep at the wheel.

You may be surprised to learn that at one time this could be used as a mitigating factor in a driver's defence; nowadays we would not accept falling asleep as a justifiable excuse, when so many tragedies happen as a result of driver sleepiness.

Road accidents where the driver had fallen asleep are more likely to result in deaths, because the vehicle is usually travelling at high speed at the time of the accident.

Accidents caused by falling asleep do not always take place at night. In fact, statistics suggest that a significant proportion of them involve long-haul business drivers operating 'on autopilot' (see previous page).

The car today has become a 'mobile office' for many people. Inside you are comfortable and warm, and cocooned from much of the exterior traffic noise, especially if you are listening to music. And whereas in the past you would need to stop and get out to make a phone call, mobile phones have made this unnecessary (although ideally you *should* stop). So it becomes more likely that you may drift off into sleep without realising it.

Research has shown that younger male drivers (aged 18–30) are more at risk of falling asleep at the wheel than other drivers. They may keep late hours and be lacking in sleep; they tend to drive fast and be over-confident of their ability; and they are less likely than, say, women driving with children, to stop and take a break.

Note: some people suffer from identifiable sleep disorders such as narcolepsy, where a person is able to carry out relatively complex tasks while dozing at the same time. If you suspect you may be a sufferer, consult your doctor to check whether you are safe to drive.

WAYS TO COMBAT THE RISKS OF DRIVER FATIGUE

- **Plan your journey** to allow for **regular breaks,** where you will get out of the car for a walk, a coffee or other refreshment (see below), and some fresh air. If you are on a motorway, make use of the service stations for this purpose – feeling sleepy is *not* counted as an 'emergency' for which you are allowed to pull on to the hard shoulder.

- **Plan your time** so that you do not drive for too long without a break. Different individuals will have different optimum periods for continuous driving, but a rough guide is to drive for no more than two hours at a stretch, which for many people is quite enough.

- **Plan your route** with the time of travel in mind, avoiding roads that you know to be congested at certain times. (See page 35 for more on route planning.)

If you know that you are one of the seven out of 10 motorists who do not feel comfortable about night driving, why not book an hour or so of tuition with an advanced driving instruc-tor? They will be able to re-inforce the points listed in this book and assist you by means of 'com-mentary driving' (see page 56).

The letters 'DWA' stand for 'driving without awareness', a term used by police to identify the risk that business drivers are exposed to when they regularly drive the same routes on long journeys.

- Becoming stressed while driving can contribute to fatigue. Take time to **concentrate your mind** on the task in hand and try to forget about other problems while driving.

- **Be aware** of the times when the urge to sleep is at its strongest. For most people, this is from midnight to 6am and from 2–4pm. This is why it is particularly dangerous to drink alcohol at lunchtime and then get back behind the wheel; the effects of the alcohol will be magnified due to tiredness.

- If you are a business traveller, find out the parts of your route where drivers are **known to be at risk** of falling asleep; for example, part of the M6 is known to police as the 'sleepy corridor'. Work out strategies for driving these routes safely.

- If you have had **insufficient sleep,** remember that you are likely to suffer from tiredness the following day.

- When you feel yourself getting sleepy, **open the windows** to let in some cold air, and **avoid driving in a tense or strained position** that could lead to headaches. **Stop and take a break** as soon as possible. Feelings of sleepiness are your body's way of warning you that you are likely to fall into a doze and thus are too tired to drive. **Don't ignore these warnings!**

- Recent research by the Sleep Research Centre at Loughborough University suggests that the most effective way to deal with sleepiness may be to have a can of a **caffeine-based drink combined with a short nap** before continuing your journey. 'Sports' or 'energy' drinks are widely available – and popular with the younger drivers known to be at higher risk.

- Some people find that chewing gum or sucking a sweet helps to keep them alert and awake.

MEDICINES AND PRESCRIPTION DRUGS

Medicinal drugs can impair driving performance. If you are taking any medicines, check with your doctor whether it is safe for you to drive.

The various effects of taking illicit drugs when driving are the subject of ongoing research, and the Government is concerned to find a simply administered test for drugs to mirror the current tests for drink-driving. But at the very least if you have taken drugs before driving, your concentration, hazard perception and reaction speed will be adversely affected, and you will be more likely to take risks.

The distance you drive is directly related to the likelihood that you will feel sleepy. In a survey of drivers who had been in accidents, only 3% of those who had driven 100 miles or less felt sleepy when the accident happened, but of those who had driven 200 miles or more, 14% admitted to having felt sleepy.

131

TEST YOUR UNDERSTANDING OF THIS SECTION

1. Some people say that they prefer driving at night to driving in the day. What reasons might they give?

2. Why should you be prepared to drive at slower speeds at night?

3. Which types of road users are particularly at risk in the dark?

4. Which groups of drivers might be at risk of falling asleep at the wheel during the day?

5. What do the letters 'DWA' stand for?

6. How should you plan your journey to avoid being overcome by tiredness?

7. How long can you safely drive without a break?

8. How can being stressed while driving contribute to the risk of falling asleep?

9. At what times of the day and night are you most at risk of falling asleep at the wheel?

10. To combat fatigue, is it best to a) go for a walk, b) open the car window, or c) have a drink?

Answers on pages 198–9

The way ahead

The way ahead

The symbols for the controls in modern cars are fairly universal, but make sure you are able to locate all the switches, as their position can vary in different models.

In this section we provide some practical advice on the challenges of driving a new or unfamiliar vehicle and on driving abroad, as well as tips on effective route planning, and how to deal with breakdowns and accidents. Looking after your vehicle, and minimising risks to security, are also covered.

DRIVING A NEW OR UNFAMILIAR VEHICLE

One occasion when you may be faced with driving an unfamiliar vehicle is if you hire a car while **travelling abroad** (see 'Driving abroad', page 138).

Another is when people **travelling on business** have to use an unfamiliar company car to attend a meeting or conference. As well as finding the way there and making mental preparations for their contribution, they have to get used to controlling the new vehicle.

Drivers have to make adjustments to their technique if they change from a **manual to an automatic** car, or from one fitted with **power-assisted steering** to one without.

If you are faced with any of these, or similar situations, make sure you allow extra time to familiarise yourself with the controls before you set out on the road.

What to look for

- Look at the **gear lever** to find out how many gears there are and how the gear changes work. The forward gears in most cars are located in the same place, but the position of **reverse** can vary in different models. Find out whether it requires, for example, a firm press down and to the left, or a lift across a 'gate' and then to the right to engage reverse.

Note: the gear selector in an automatic car looks very different (see diagram, page 81). As well as the familiar forward and reverse gears, you will find Park and Drive. (See page 136 for start-up and driving techniques for automatic vehicles.)

- Consult the vehicle's **manual** to find out as much as you can about the **controls** – including **auxiliary controls.** Make sure you will know the meaning of any **warning lights** that might come on.

- Locate the switches for the **indicators, lights** and **windscreen wipers.** Check on how to select:

position lights/dipped headlights/main beam or 'flash'; fog lights and hazard warning lights; intermittent/regular/ double-speed wipers.

- Remember to **adjust the seats, the door and rear view mirrors and the head restraints** to the correct heights and angles *before* you start driving.

- Check the vehicle carefully for damage before you use it, including the tyres for wear, cuts and bulges.

- Check that there is a spare tyre and that it is inflated, and that the jack and other tools are present.

Even if you only intend to drive the vehicle in daylight, you need to be clear on how to use the lights in case of poor visibility.

Don't forget to check whether the vehicle has a rear windscreen wiper, and how to operate this.

(If you accept a hire car with anything missing, you may be charged with their cost when you return the car.)

- Check the Road Fund Licence (or tax disk) is current.

- Check the windscreen for chips and cracking.

- Find out what type of **fuel** the vehicle takes – and how to open the fuel cap.

- Find out how the **alarm system** is activated and de-activated.

- When hiring a car, make sure you know what to do in the event of a **breakdown,** and what **insurance** cover you and your passengers have while using the vehicle.

- If you have hired a **four-wheel-drive** vehicle and you have not driven one before, study the manual carefully for advice on when and when not to engage four-wheel-drive. (Using four-wheel-drive when it is not needed can waste fuel. For more on four-wheel-drive and off-road driving, see pages 19–20.)

Driving an automatic vehicle

In an automatic vehicle there are only **two pedals** (accelerator and brake), and different techniques are used to control the car from those used in a manually controlled vehicle.

You should use your **right** foot to operate **both** of the pedals.

To start the vehicle, the gear lever must be in either **park** or **neutral.** When you have started the engine, place your right foot **on the brake.**

Select **drive** and slowly lift your foot off the brake, moving it to the accelerator as the vehicle picks up speed. The automatic transmission will change the gears up as you accelerate and down as you brake.

TEST YOUR UNDERSTANDING
OF THIS SECTION

1. What aspects of the vehicle should you attempt to familiarise yourself with before starting to drive?

2. Why might you find it useful to read through the manual before driving a new or unfamiliar vehicle?

3. How do the gears and pedals of an automatic car differ from those of a manual car?

Answers on page 199–200

Driving abroad

A driving instructor's tip: add a mirror for your passenger's use, so that they can give you some help until you feel confident. Most accidents that happen to people who are driving abroad for the first time take place within the first 50 miles.

Driving abroad can be somewhat daunting on the first occasion, especially if you also have to get used to **an unfamiliar hire car** and learn how to **drive on the right.**

However, after a couple of hours' experience you should feel quite confident – and on subsequent occasions you will find you adapt very quickly. Every time you leave a car park or a one-way street, check which side of the road you should be using.

RESEARCH YOUR DESTINATION

You can make the experience easier and more pleasant if you have 'done your homework' before you go.

Find out as much as you can about the traffic regulations and road signs in the country you are going to. The AA can provide detailed information on many destinations, and AA members will find an up-to-date summary of advice in their handbook.

Here are some suggestions for what to check up on before you set off.

DRIVING ABROAD AND *THE HIGHWAY CODE*

In the UK not all of the *The Highway Code* is a **legal requirement,** but this is not the case elsewhere, and you will be **committing a criminal offence** if you infringe any part of the equivalent of *The Highway Code* in the country you are visiting.

So, for example, breaking the **speed limit** could land you in serious trouble. You should be aware that in many countries the penalty is a very expensive **on the spot fine.** (And in Germany, for example, you can also be charged with vagrancy, if you do not carry sufficient cash to pay the fine on the spot.)

SPEED LIMIT SIGNS

- A list of speed limits is usually displayed at border crossings in Europe, but there may be **no subsequent reminders,** so you should take careful note when you see them.

- In some areas of France and Germany, the speed limit is indicated not by a speed limit sign but by a **place-name** sign.

Additional restrictions

- As in the UK, the speed limits given are the **maximum** and you should adjust your speed as appropriate for wet weather, fog etc. Again, driving at a lower speed in adverse weather conditions may be a **legal requirement** (as it is in France), and not just a safety measure.

- Check on whether **newly qualified drivers** are restricted to lower speeds. For example, drivers who have held a licence for less than two years are restricted to lower speeds when driving in France.

- Check the local regulations about **carrying children:** in some countries, children under a certain age or size are not permitted to travel in the front seat of a vehicle.

GENERAL RULES

- Find out as much as you can about the motoring laws in the country you are visiting. For example, what are the rules about **pedestrian crossings?** Must you stop for a person already on the crossing, as in the UK, or are the crossings strictly controlled by lights?

- On two-way roads in the USA, all vehicles must stop when a **school bus** is taking on or letting off passengers. On dual carriageways this regulation applies only to traffic going in the same direction as the bus. Severe penalties apply if you break the rules.

- In Hungary, drivers must keep their headlights on **at all times** outside built-up areas, even in fine weather. This is also the case in Canada, since you can never be sure when you will drive into an unexpected patch of fog. In Scandinavian countries, car headlights must be on whenever the car is on the road.

- Many countries have rules about **carrying alcohol** in the vehicle; check in the information pages of your travel guide for the rules in your destination.

Find out what the local name is for the motorway; autoroute, autostrada and rapida are some examples. The signs for motorways tend to be familiar international signs.

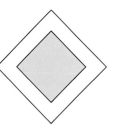 

When driving on the right, many people find that they need to take special care when passing parked cars – it's easy to drive too close to them. And you may find it confusing when you negotiate your first roundabout in what feels like the wrong direction.

● Remember that the **condition of roads** may be very different from what you are used to, and you may have to negotiate sizeable potholes and drive on extremely rough surfaces. In Australia, for example, minor roads are often 'unsealed' – this means they do not have a tarmac surface, and may become impassible in the wet season due to flooding. You should always take local advice before proceeding, and check that the road is appropriate for saloon cars if you do not have a four-wheel-drive vehicle. You may even find that your hire-car insurance does not cover you to drive on certain roads.

● Although the British have the dubious distinction of exhibiting the highest incidence of 'road rage', you may not be aware that in Germany, the second country in the 'road rage' stakes, making an 'offensive' gesture can lead to a **fine.**

● When planning your route, make sure you have an up-to-date copy of a **good road atlas** for the country you are visiting. For example, you will find lots of useful information in the introductory pages of the AA's *Big Road Atlas Europe.*

● If you are a member of a motoring organisation, check the terms and conditions of your breakdown cover, to see whether they allow for **recovery of your vehicle** to the UK in the event of a breakdown.

● Find out about any unfamiliar conventions about **who has priority** (such as **giving priority to traffic coming from the right**), and how these are signed. Watch out for **cyclists,** who may have priority where a cycle track crosses a road, and for **trams,** which cannot swerve to avoid you.

● Remember that a **'STOP'** sign means just that.

In the UK you may sometimes keep the car moving at a slow speed if you can see that it is safe to proceed at a junction, but in most other countries you are required to bring the car to a **complete** stop before proceeding.

The following signs may be found in Europe. the yellow diamond means a priority route, the red circle means slow down and keep your distance, while the blue circle means snow chains may be required.

TOLLS

Many countries charge a toll for using the motorways, and you will find it helpful to have prior knowledge about these.

Toll booths in some countries (such as France and Spain) accept major **credit cards,** but not travellers' cheques. In some places you must buy a **card** in advance, such as the 'Viacard' used in Italy, otherwise you will need the correct amount in the **local currency.**

DOCUMENTS

Keep all your documents in a safe place, and readily available for inspection if necessary as the practice of spot checks on foreign cars is widespread.

You should have with you:

● Passports and visas

● Driving Licence

● International Driving Permit (see below)

● Vehicle Registration Document (original, not a photocopy)

● Insurance documents (vehicle and travel)

International Driving Permit (IDP)

This document, which can be obtained from selected main post offices, is required in addition to your driving licence when travelling in some countries.

You can find out whether you need one from the AA's website at www.theAA.com.

It is advisable to obtain one if your driving licence is not the 'photocard' type, since the police will often expect to see a form of identification that includes your photo, as well as

Before you take your car abroad you should inform your insurers, who will extend your full home cover while you are away.

Some of the items listed here under Spares and Equipment such as a First Aid kit, spare bulbs and warning triangles, are compulsory in some countries, such as Spain, and if you do not carry them you could be liable for a fine.

your driving licence. (For more on IDP's, see the 'Answers' section on page 201.)

Check carefully before you leave on what is and is not covered in your **travel insurance,** and make amendments if necessary. If you make more than one trip abroad during a year, you will probably find that annual travel insurance provides you with the best range of cover for the most economical price.

SPARES AND EQUIPMENT

Here are some of the items you will find it useful to carry in your car.

- First Aid kit (see page 164)

- Spare bulbs

- Warning triangle (see page 164)

- Spare tyre

- Spare set of keys (don't leave them in the car!)

- Tool kit and jack

- Maps and atlases

- Snow chains where appropriate

- Drinking water

You may need to display a **GB sticker** (International Distinguishing Sign) of the approved size and type at the rear of your vehicle, and also on your

caravan or trailer if you have one.

The sticker should be elliptical in shape with black letters on a white ground. The sticker must be at least 175mm in width and 115mm in height, and the letters a minimum of 80mm high and 10mm wide.

Since March 2001 it has been a **legal option** to display the GB Euro-symbol on UK registration plates, making display of a conventional GB sticker unnecessary within the EU. The plates must comply with British Standard BSAU145d, and you are advised to continue to display a GB sticker alongside the Euro-plate when travelling outside the EU.

ALLOWANCES

Make sure you know what you are allowed to bring back to the UK with you.

- You can bring back into the UK as many EU duty-paid goods as you like, provided these are for your personal use.

- But if you bring back goods for other people and accept payment for them, you are liable to pay the full UK duty and tax.

The amounts considered reasonable for personal consumption by Customs and Excise are as follows:

- Cigarettes 800

- Cigarillos 400

- Cigars 200

- Tobacco 1kg

- Spirits 10 litres

- Fortified wine (such as sherry, port) 20 litres

- Wine 90 litres (including not more than 60 litres of sparkling wine)

- Beer 110 litres

If you are challenged, you will have to convince the Customs Officer that all items are for your own consumption, otherwise the goods and your vehicle may be confiscated.

Smuggling

The current policy means that anyone caught smuggling can expect that their vehicle will be confiscated **permanently.**

If you lend your vehicle to someone who then uses it for smuggling, your vehicle will be seized even though you were not responsible.

DISTANCE CONVERSIONS

KMS	KMS/MILES	MILES
1.6	1	0.6
3.2	2	1.2
4.8	3	1.9
6.4	4	2.5
8.1	5	3.1
9.7	6	3.7
11.3	7	4.4
12.9	8	5.0
14.5	9	5.6
16.1	10	6.2
32.2	20	12.4
48.3	30	18.6
64.4	40	24.9
80.5	50	31.1
160.9	100	62.1

TEST YOUR UNDERSTANDING OF THIS SECTION

1. What are some of the problems you might expect to encounter when driving on the right for the first time?

2. When travelling to a country you have not visited before, what information should you try to find out in advance?

3. What should you be aware of with regard to speed limits abroad?

4. On what kinds of roads would you expect to pay toll charges?

5. Which documents must you have with you in your vehicle?

6. Why might it be advisable to obtain an International Driving Permit (IDP?)

7. What spares and other equipment is it advisable to carry in your vehicle in case of emergency?

8. How can you find out about allowances for bringing back goods from abroad?

Answers on pages 200–2

Loading your vehicle

The regulations regarding vehicle loading are varied and complex, depending on the type of vehicle. What follows is a brief overview of the general rules for loading goods and passengers.

You should be aware that **overloading can significantly affect the steering and handling of your vehicle.** This is especially noticeable when negotiating bends, or changing direction.

Too much weight in the back of the vehicle can have an adverse effect on **braking.**

You may need to inflate your tyres to more than the normal pressures if you are carrying a heavy load (always check your car's manual); for example, when you have more than three passengers on board. This is not done with the aim of giving a smoother ride to your passengers, but to ensure that the extra weight does not cause more of the tyre surface to come in contact with the road. When that happens, tyres can become over-heated, and there is a risk of blow-outs.

- Load heavy items as close to the centre of the car as possible, and keep the weight as close to the floor as possible.

- When loading the boot, ensure that the weight is **evenly distributed.** Loading the heaviest objects at the rear (near the bumper) will adversely affect the vehicle's handling.

A useful tip is to load only a few large objects over the spare tyre, so that they are easily removed if you need to fit the spare during your journey.

Any vehicle towing a trailer must have lights showing if it is parked overnight. This also applies to unattached trailers.

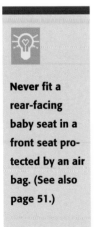

Never fit a rear-facing baby seat in a front seat protected by an air bag. (See also page 51.)

THE DRIVER'S RESPONSIBILITY

- You should be aware that as the driver, **you** have responsibility for ensuring that your vehicle is not overloaded – not the owner of the vehicle (if it is not you), or the person who loaded it.

- You are responsible for seeing that **passengers** are securely seated in the most suitable part of the vehicle, and that all passengers wear the correct **seat belts or restraints** (see below).

- If you are using a roof rack, your load must be **secured and must not stick out dangerously.** You should make allowances for the fact that a roof rack is likely to affect the stability of the vehicle.

- You must not **tow** any load greater than **permitted by your licence.**

- If you tow a caravan or trailer, make sure the load is **evenly distributed** to prevent 'snaking' and loss of control. Heavy items should be loaded as low in the caravan as possible, and mainly over the axle(s).

- When carrying **bicycles** on a suitable rack on the back of the vehicle, **you must not block the vehicle's lights or number plates.** A good tip is to attach a separate towing board fitted with lights and number plates and connected to the towing socket.

- Safely stow or tie down loose items in the passenger compartment. In the event of a collision, they will act as a missile when projected forward.

PASSENGERS

All adult passengers must wear seat belts unless medically exempt, and children under 14 must be secured in a child seat, or wear a restraint appropriate to their age. A detailed list of appropriate restraints can be found in *The Highway Code.*

Children must not be allowed to sit in the space behind the back seat of an estate car or hatchback, and passengers are not allowed in a caravan while it is being towed. You should not allow an adult to sit holding a child on their knee.

Pets should be conveyed in an approved and safe manner in your vehicle. A harness designed to be held secure by fastening through the seat belt is available for dogs. Large dogs should be in a secure area at the rear of a hatchback, with a screen to prevent them being thrown forward in an accident.

TEST YOUR UNDERSTANDING OF THIS SECTION

1. If you are carrying too heavy a load, when is it most likely to affect the handling of your vehicle?

2. Whose responsibility is it to check that a vehicle is not overloaded?

3. How can you find out what size of load you are permitted to tow?

4. If your children become bored while travelling to a holiday caravan site, is it acceptable for them to sit in the caravan and play card games?

Answers on page 202

Getting to know your vehicle

Make sure you know which lights alert you to stop immediately. For example, if the oil light comes on and you continue driving, you will cause irreparable damage to the engine. A red ignition warning light together with a rapid rise in engine temperature could indicate a broken drive belt – again, you need to stop immediately and investigate.

How much does an 'expert' driver need to know about the workings of their vehicle?

Nowadays there is no need for concern if you do not have a great desire to acquire in-depth technical knowledge about the mechanics of your vehicle. Tasks such as stripping a gearbox or engine are best left to experts at your garage, and many components are now fitted as sealed units, which do not lend themselves to investigation by amateurs.

It *is* advisable, however, to get to know your own vehicle to the extent that you can deal with daily routine maintenance, and identify when something needs attention; for example, when there is a change in the engine noise, or an unexpected loss of acceleration, or if the brakes do not feel 'right'. You should also pay prompt attention to any warning lights on the dashboard display panel.

Have your vehicle **serviced regularly,** and keep the written record of service up-to-date.

Carry out **regular checks;** the main ones are listed below.

CHECKS YOU CAN DO YOURSELF

Oil

This should be done before you start the engine, and preferably after the vehicle has been standing for several hours. Make sure you are parked on a level road surface when you do the check.

Pull out the dipstick and wipe it with a cloth; put it back in as far as it will go, then pull it out again – the oil level should come between half way and the 'full' markers. Add some engine oil if it's low, pouring it through the filler cap. Some high-performance engines may require a non-standard oil – check your car's manual.

Tyres

Tyres should be visually checked for **damage** (for example, resulting from kerb impact) and for **wear.**

TYRE PRESSURES

At least once a fortnight, all the tyres (including the spare) should be checked with a tyre pressure gauge. A footpump with a dial gauge is suitable, but always check that the needle starts from 'zero'. A pencil-type gauge is probably more reliable. With the tyres cold (that is, not just after driving), unscrew each valve cap in turn and firmly apply the gauge head.

Note: some gauges will grip the tyre valve, but most need to be held in place manually, and must be held at the same angle as the tyre valve so as not to lose air.

Check the gauge reading against the car handbook, or the label on the edge of the driver's door frame. Front and rear are usually different, and there may be increases recommended for extra loads.

Correct the pressure with a foot pump or garage air-line if necessary, then refit the valve cap. If more than a few pounds of pressure have been lost, have the tyre checked and repaired.

TREAD DEPTH

Make a point of watching the tyre tread depth, which must be at least 1.6mm all the way around the tyre.

In wet conditions, grip drops dramatically when it's less than 2mm, so renew before this limit is reached. Look out for cuts, bulges or uneven wear.

Lights

Before you set out, check that all lights are working; this is especially important at night, when you may be tired and liable to forget. If possible, get someone to help you check that your brake lights are working; alternatively, park close to a reflective surface, such as a garage door, and check you can see each light reflected. Check the reversing lights with the engine off, ignition on, and reverse gear selected.

Front and rear screens

Ensure that these are clean and free from grease. Inspect the front windscreen for damage – particularly in the driver's line of sight. Replace any faulty wiper blades. Keep a clean soft cloth in the vehicle in case you need to clean the screens again later.

Note: bright sunlight can react with plastics used in the manufacture of your vehicle's interior trim; chemicals can leak out, forcing a microscopic vapour that collects on the inside of the windscreen. So remember to clean the **inside** as well

When you check the tread depth, look each tyre over carefully. Misalignment can lead to uneven tyre wear. Don't forget to check the spare tyre as well. *The Highway Code states a minimum tread depth of 1.6mm, but 2mm is a safer guide.*

as the outside of the windscreen regularly.

Screen wash

It is a legal requirement that you keep an adequate level of screen wash to clear your screen in adverse weather. It is best to use a prepared screen wash from a garage or motor accessory shop rather than washing-up liquid, which can cause smearing. Good screen cleaners contain additives that stop the screen from icing up in winter, and prevent dead insects from sticking to it in summer. It is a legal requirement that it **MUST NOT** freeze up in winter.

Fuel gauge

It is surprising how many breakdown service call-outs are to motorists who have simply run out of fuel. Check that you have enough before you start your journey, and fill up if necessary.

CHECKS TO HAVE DONE AT YOUR GARAGE

The garage will normally check and replace all filters; check the EMS (see page 51) electronically; replace or replenish all fluids; and inspect or replace brakes. However, the level of checking may depend on the mileage of the vehicle, and what you ask for.

Battery

The terminals should be cleaned and protected from corrosion at every service. The battery is likely to need replacing after about five years.

Distributor cap

Moisture and dirt can damage this vital ignition component in older vehicles. A scarcely visible crack in the insulation can allow high ignition voltages to leak away, resulting in no ignition spark. Your garage should check to see if the cap, or its weather-protective covering, needs replacing.

Clutch cable

The clutch cable is under high stress, and abrasion can weaken the wire strands in the cable until it breaks. Temporary repairs can often be made at the roadside, but replacement of the cable at the first signs of wear is the best answer.

Spark plugs

Plugs should be replaced at the manufacturer's recommended service interval.

HT leads

High-tension leads and their connections can deteriorate with age, when water and dirt enter cracks in the insulation, reducing ignition voltage. Damp-repellent sprays are only a temporary solution, so your garage should check the condition of the leads, and replace as necessary. Some types of HT leads need to be replaced every 25,000 miles.

Engine Management Systems

Modern cars are fitted with computerised engine management systems (EMS). Your garage should be equipped with computer diagnostic equipment to discover faults – leave it to them!

ON THE ROAD

Many people choose to join a motoring organisation such as the AA to give them peace of mind in the event of a breakdown. (See breakdown advice, below.) However, you will probably want to have sufficient knowledge and ability to change a wheel yourself if you choose not to call out a breakdown organisation. Practise in advance so that you will not be faced with changing the wheel for the first time in a stressful situation.

● Check that the spare wheel, jack, wheelbrace and wheel chock are in the car and in good working condition. Wheel nuts can be difficult to loosen: a good quality

wheelbrace at least 500mm in length is recommended. After a wheel change, the correct setting of the nuts (or studs) must be checked with a torque wrench – a garage or specialist tyre-fitter can do this for you.

● If your vehicle is fitted with locking wheel nuts, make sure the key or removal tool is available for use.

● **Do not attempt to change a wheel or carry out any other repairs at the roadside or the hard shoulder of a motorway.** Find a safe stopping place before you begin.

What to do if you break down

The last point listed above forms part of the AA's advice to motorists on how to proceed safely in the event of a breakdown.

Remember your checks:

P = petrol (fuel)

O = oil

W = water

E = electrics (lights, indicators etc)

R = rubber (tyres, wiper blades)

It is all too easy to fill up a **diesel** car with **petrol** (or vice versa) by mistake. (39,000 AA members did so in one year.) Take care not to do this, as the car would need to be recovered to a garage to have the tank drained and the contents disposed of – a costly mistake.

Other points to bear in mind include:

- Try to get your vehicle into a safe place off the road.

- Switch on hazard warning lights.

- If you cannot get your vehicle clear of the road and you have a warning triangle, place it at least 100m behind your vehicle to warn oncoming traffic. (Do not place a warning triangle on a motorway.)

- Get all passengers out of the vehicle to a safe place until help arrives. If you are on a motorway, this should be behind the barrier, on the bank or verge. Leave animals in the vehicle with ventilation. If you feel vulnerable, you should remain inside the vehicle with doors locked and with your seatbelt fastened until help arrives, or until you feel the danger has passed.

- Telephone your breakdown organisation or the emergency services. If on the motorway, use the emergency phone.

- Remain with your vehicle if you have summoned breakdown assistance, as patrols are not allowed to work on unaccompanied vehicles. If you are fortunate enough to get going again before they arrive, be sure to telephone the breakdown organisation to let them know.

TEST YOUR UNDERSTANDING OF THIS SECTION

1. Why should you stop immediately if a red oil light comes on?

2. What should you bear in mind when preparing to check your oil level?

3. What should the tread depth be on your tyres?

4. How can you check that your rear lights are working?

5. What are some of the checks that you should expect your garage to make as part of regular services?

6. Is it correct procedure to switch on your hazard warning lights when you break down?

Answers on page 203

Route planning

Choose a 'maxi-scale' atlas if you prefer a large scale of mapping, and decide whether a spiral-bound or standard version is most appropriate for your needs.

Being an expert driver means that you are just as good at finding your way around as you are at controlling the car.

Some people are blessed with a better sense of direction than others, but you can improve your basic directional ability through planning, concentration and experience. For example, you can teach yourself to find your way towards the centre of a town, or away from it, by learning to recognise visual clues – such as that a long road filled with guest houses usually marks a radial route in and out of a town. Being aware of the position of the sun may also help you to know your general direction.

There are several choices of navigation aids available to drivers; some of them are discussed in this section. But the key to success is careful **planning.**

If you are contemplating a long or unfamiliar journey, set time aside to look up the best route on a map, note the possible problem points, and make a detailed list of all the major towns and junctions along the way (see page 35), in the order you'll pass through them.

If you are travelling with a passenger, they can read the directions out to you and keep an eye on the map; but if you are on your own, you might prefer to make a tape of your route directions to play back as you drive.

When you plan your route, remember to **plan an alternative** also; for example, the motorway junction you planned to take might be closed, and you would have to adapt your plan accordingly.

Be prepared to pull up in a safe place to check your route. You cannot stop for this on a motorway – expect to leave the motorway at the next junction to check your route, or pull in at a service station.

EFFECTIVE MAP READING

Here are some suggestions for making the best use of your map or atlas.

- Check that the map you are using is **up-to-date.** Confusion and time-wasting can result when, for example, a new by-pass has been built that alters the course of the route but does not appear on your map, or road numbers have been altered.

- If you plan to use a road atlas, select one that is **clear and easy to read** (the example below is from an AA road atlas).

Remember that even the best maps and atlases are limited in how much detail they can display. For example, all but the most complex round-abouts are usually shown as a circle, which may not give you much of a clue about how large or busy they are.

If you are driving in very remote areas, leave a copy of your route directions with someone else, as a safeguard in the event of breaking down.

- Make sure you know how to **identify the main features** on the maps, such as the different types of roads, and how roundabouts, junctions and landscape features are shown. Some motorway exits are available in one direction only; notice how this is indicated (typically, with the number shown in red or yellow).

- Study the page headed '**Key to map symbols**', so that you become familiar with these and do not waste time puzzling over them during your journey.

- If you are not sure how to use the **grid references** in the index to locate places on your map, study the explanation.

Other ways of obtaining traffic and travel information

You can telephone a service such as **AA Roadwatch** for information on your route and listen to local and national **radio** stations for regular traffic news on major routes.

Other databases collate information about traffic movements from sources such as traffic flow sensors positioned over the carriageway, police and local authority databases, and public transport companies.

This information can then be relayed to the driver through a recorded message or a 'live' operator.

Drivers can also receive additional customised information relevant to their destination, such as hotel accommodation in the area they are visiting, or the locations of car parks or bank cash points.

Most systems are designed to work wherever you travel throughout Europe, while continuing to relay information in your own language.

NEW POSSIBILITIES – IN-CAR TELEMATICS

'Telematics' is the term used to refer to wireless communication information services for drivers in their vehicles.

Telematics differs from radio broadcasting because the information is '**dynamic**'.

- The information delivered is directly relevant to the driver's needs because it is **location-based.**

- Telematics allows for the possibility of two-way communication between the driver and the provider(s) of the information service.

- The information can be 'tailored' to the requirements of the individual motorist, or manager of a fleet of business vehicles, who has requested it.

How does it work?

At the time of writing several different systems are in development, and there is much debate about the best and safest way to deliver the information (this is an area where safety issues and the development of cost-effective technology may sometimes conflict – see page 158).

RELAYING THE VEHICLE'S POSITION TO THE BASE

A **GPS** (Global Positioning System) unit installed in the vehicle relays its precise position on the Earth's surface to a satellite, which transmits the data back to a collection unit on the ground. The data can be viewed on a computer screen in the form of a position on a digital map.

Once the information on the vehicle's position has been received at the base, it can be used in many different ways in addition to providing route guidance and traffic information. For example, help can be despatched in the event of an accident or breakdown; the telematics system has the capacity to identify and locate mechanical faults; and a stolen car can be located with the help of telematics.

TELEMATICS AND FLEET VEHICLES

The technology of telematics systems is attractive to fleet managers because it has the potential to make the time people spend in their car more profitable to the employer.

When a substantial proportion of an employee's day is spent driving, much potential work time can be lost, especially when there are long delays due to traffic congestion, roadworks, etc.

Vehicle tracking systems make it possible for managers to monitor the movements of their workforce, ensure schedules are followed, and transmit advice on alternative routes – all ways of saving time and money for the company.

A NOTE OF CAUTION

The most effective telematics systems rely on hardware that is built into the vehicle (including a GPS unit, a cellular phone chip and a voice recognition system). However, this is at present very expensive, so some systems rely instead on mobile phones, the risks of which are discussed elsewhere (see page 118).

Although the cost of telematics hardware may fall as it becomes more widely adopted, there is still the significant risk of **driver distraction,** even when a hands-free system is used. Some potential developments should therefore be viewed with caution, such as the possibility of logging on to the internet, or sending voice-activated e-mails, while in the car.

TEST YOUR UNDERSTANDING
OF THIS SECTION

1. What should you bear in mind when planning your route for a long or unfamiliar journey?

2. How can you make the most effective use of your road atlas?

3. In what ways could telematics aid the business driver?

4. Why should drivers exercise extra care when using a voice-operated system?

Answers on page 204

Road signs – updating your knowledge

A survey timed to commemorate the 70th anniversary of the publication of *The Highway Code* found that more than 50 per cent of drivers do not know the meanings of many common road signs. Two-thirds of those questioned admitted that they had never opened a copy of *The Highway Code* since passing their driving test as long as 40 years before.

For example:

Some people thought that this sign meant 'foot and mouth infected area'.

In fact, it warns you to look out for cattle crossing the road.

This sign was thought by some to mean 'ferry terminal ahead'.

It actually means 'quayside or riverbank'.

This sign was recognised as 'vineyard ahead'.

It means 'dual carriageway ends'.

And this sign was widely misunderstood as meaning 'one-way street ahead'.

It means 'give way to oncoming vehicles'.

Road and traffic signs were updated in the Traffic Signs Regulations (1994), when many new signs were introduced and changes were also made to existing designs.

If you would like to read a full (and quite entertaining) account of the history of traffic signs, obtain a copy of *Know Your Traffic Signs* (published by TSO).

For now, test your knowledge of the following signs; their meanings are given in the Answers section of this book on page 205.

1

5

2

6

3

4

Many of the newer road signs are those giving information on **motorways,** so newly-qualified drivers would be well advised to take careful note of all the information devices that are now found positioned above the carriageway and on the central reservation.

Signs instructing you to **move to the opposite carriageway** can be complex and sometimes confusing. Study the examples illustrated towards the end of *The Highway Code* in order to become more familiar with these contraflow direction signs.

What to do in an accident
– basic First Aid

If you are the first person to arrive at the scene of a road accident you will want to offer any assistance you can.

Your first action should be to **call the emergency services** – or get someone else to do so if you do not have access to a phone.

Study the information on accidents and First Aid in *The Highway Code* and commit it to memory. Here are some general guidelines.

- Remain calm and assess the situation.

- Ensure safety at the scene by controlling the traffic and checking that engines are switched off.

- Summon medical help if this has not already been done.

- Do not give casualties anything to eat or drink, or offer them a cigarette.

- Reassure any injured person and keep them warm while waiting for the ambulance to arrive.

- Do not move casualties unless you can see that they are in immediate danger.

- If the casualty is not breathing, lay the person on their back, lift the chin and tilt their head backwards; make sure nothing in the person's mouth is obstructing their breathing; pinch the nostrils and blow into the mouth until the chest rises. Repeat every four seconds until the person can breathe unaided. If the person is trapped in the car, tilt their head back gently to open the airway and follow the same procedure.

- If the casualty is breathing but unconscious, use the recovery position; turn the person on to his or her side, tilted slightly forward with the uppermost leg and arm bent to help prop the upper body.

- Treat severe bleeding by applying continuous direct pressure. Raise the affected limb if appropriate.

- Do not allow accident victims to wander about, even if not obviously injured – they may be **in shock** and wander into danger.

To be confident that you could be of help in an accident, consider taking a course in First Aid from St John Ambulance or St Andrew's Ambulance Association, or from the British Red Cross. You can find local contact numbers in the phone book.

Do not move an injured motorcyclist unless they are in immediate danger – they may have a neck injury. If you have to remove the helmet (see tip, right), you will need two people, one supporting the head and neck while the other lifts the helmet clear. The head and neck must be supported until a surgical collar can be fitted.

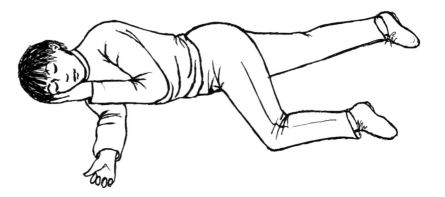

FIRST AID KITS

These are available from garages and motor accessory stores and chemists; you can buy one with the contents ready assembled, or make up your own. It makes good sense to keep a First Aid kit in your vehicle, as well as a fire extinguisher; know how to use it, and remember to re-stock the kit as necessary.

ACCIDENTS WHERE YOU ARE INVOLVED

If you are unfortunate enough to be involved in a road accident, you should **stop** and **pull off the road** into a safe place.

If this is impossible, switch on your **hazard warning lights** and place your **red warning triangle** at least 45 metres (150 feet) behind your vehicle on the same side of the road.

Note: never use a warning triangle on a motorway.

Observe all the **safety procedures** outlined above.

Stand in a **safe place** while awaiting help – not between your car and oncoming traffic. If you have stopped on the hard shoulder of a motorway, stand on the adjoining land behind the safety barrier.

Do not attempt to do any repairs to your vehicle on the carriageway.

Legal requirements

If you were involved in an accident, would you know the legal requirements for how to proceed?

The AA gives the following advice, but accompanied by a warning that it is only a summary.

If you are involved in an accident and

- someone else is injured

- damage occurs to another vehicle or to property

- a reportable animal is killed or injured (that is, dog, cow, horse, goat, pig, donkey but not others; the RSPCA should be informed if another animal is injured)

you must

- stop, and remain at the scene for a reasonable period of time

- give your vehicle registration number, your name and address and that of the vehicle's owner (if different) to anyone with reasonable grounds for requesting them

- if you do not give your name and address at the time of the accident, report the accident to the police as soon as is reasonably practicable and in any case within 24 hours.

If another person is injured, you must additionally

- produce your insurance certificate at the scene if required by anyone with reasonable grounds for requesting it. If

you do not, then you must

- report the accident to the police as soon as possible, and in any case within 24 hours

- produce your insurance certificate for the police within seven days.

Note: you must report the accident in person.

Note also: it is a condition of all vehicle insurance policies that you report any accident to your insurance company within a reasonable time.

You may find it useful to make a record of what happened while it is still clear in your mind. Note down the time, date and an account of what happened, with details of other drivers involved and any witnesses. Make a **sketch** of the position of vehicles on the road – or if you have a camera with you, take a photograph. **Record** the road markings and traffic signs at or around the accident scene, and also the weather conditions. If you need to make an insurance claim, it will be useful to have some evidence of whether the road surface was muddy, wet or icy. Remember to **sign and date** your record, and keep it for future reference.

If an injured motorcyclist is breathing and not in danger of choking, leave the helmet on. However, if the rider is unconscious and not breathing, their brain will start to die from oxygen starvation within four minutes, so you must remove the helmet to permit resuscitation.

TEST YOUR UNDERSTANDING OF THIS SECTION

1. Why must you check that no one is smoking at an accident scene?

2. Why should you not offer an injured person anything to drink?

3. What should you do to help an injured person who is not breathing?

4. What kind of training can you take in order to be of more help to others in the event of an accident?

5. If you are involved in an accident, what is the first thing you should do?

6. At an accident scene, who has a right to ask you for your details?

7. How soon after the accident must you report it to the police?

8. Why might it be helpful to draw a diagram of the accident scene?

Answers on pages 205–6

Security and your vehicle

The security of a vehicle, its passengers and contents is an important concern for all drivers.

Here are some suggestions on how you can minimise risks to people and property.

- Put personal possessions **out of sight** – perhaps in a locked boot.

- Keep your **keys** in a safe place and whenever you leave the vehicle, remove the keys from the ignition and **lock the car.**

- When you leave your vehicle, make sure that all the **windows** are fully closed and check the **sunroof.** (Never leave children on their own in a car. Even in a very short time, there's a danger of the handbrake being released and the car rolling, or other controls being moved. A car interior can overheat dangerously within a few minutes in bright weather – it doesn't have to be hot sun. Don't leave pets in the car without adequate ventilation.)

- Think about your **personal safety** as part of your journey planning (see page 154). Consider whether you would be at risk if you were to break down in a remote area, and decide what steps you can take to ensure you are less vulnerable. (See also page 151.)

It pays to lock your car even when going to pay for fuel at the garage.

Take note of buildings in the area around your chosen parking place; for example, if you park in a street close to a cinema or sports stadium, people may stream past your car on their way out and may damage your car, whether deliberately or not.

If your vehicle has central locking, this gives you the option of locking all doors temporarily if you feel vulnerable.

Information about immobilisation devices can be obtained from the Vehicle Security National Helpline on 0870 5502006.

- Consider whether you would want to **lock doors when the vehicle is in motion** as well as when it is stationary. In town driving, one view holds that locking the doors protects you from criminals who may try to snatch open the door while you are stationary at traffic lights, grabbing a handbag or rifling through the glove compartment. On the other hand, on a motorway, where collisions are likely to be a more serious risk, and it would be more difficult to get passengers out quickly in an accident, you may prefer not to lock your doors.

- Be careful if you decide to **lend your vehicle** to anyone else. Make sure that you are fully confident they will look after it properly, and not use it for illicit purposes. (See also page 143 – if anyone else were to use your vehicle to smuggle prohibited goods into the country, it would be impounded.) Check your insurance cover, too.

- Try to **park in a safe place.** If possible park under a street light, and avoid areas where there are few other vehicles. Multi-storey car parks can be the safest place in a town to park, or they can be quite the reverse – rely on local knowledge to guide you.

CRIME DETERRENCE

In addition to the precautions listed above, the Driver Vehicle Licensing Agency (DVLA) offers some specific suggestions for reducing vehicle crime.

- Fit an **immobiliser** to the engine and some other more obvious deterent such as a steering wheel lock.

- Have the vehicle's **registration number etched** on all glass surfaces – including headlights. You could also use the last seven digits of the Vehicle Identification Number (VIN), or a unique number linked to an authorised database.

- Consider **marking all valuables** carried in your car with a unique number as above, or with your postcode.

- Fit a **removable stereo,** or one with a front that can be taken off. The stereo should also be marked for identification.

- Fit **locking wheel nuts** to protect your wheels and tyres.

TEST YOUR UNDERSTANDING OF THIS SECTION

1. What can you do to minimise the risk of theft from your vehicle?

2. Why should you exercise care about lending your vehicle to someone else?

3. What should you bear in mind when selecting a place to park?

4. How can etching your registration number on the glass surfaces of your vehicle help in combating crime?

Answers on page 206

A postscript on re-testing

More than 30 police forces have adopted the National Driver Improvement Scheme for re-training offenders.

Should your driving test be the *only* assessment of your ability throughout your driving career, or should there be further tests at intervals to make sure you are still competent?

At the time of writing this is the subject of much debate; older drivers are one group under discussion (see pages 36–9). The Government supports any initiative that will promote a culture of safer driving, and re-testing is one option.

At present there are two distinct examples of driver re-testing: voluntary assessment and re-testing imposed by a court of law.

VOLUNTARY ASSESSMENT

People who undertake courses with the Institute of Advanced Motorists often choose to prepare for a certificate to prove their competence by passing the IAM Advanced Driving Test (see page 16). This is undertaken for their own satisfaction and perhaps to reduce insurance costs.

Driver improvement courses arranged by companies for their employees can also lead to a written record of competence.

RE-TESTING AS A PENALTY IMPOSED BY THE COURTS

Since 1992, drivers who have been disqualified for serious driving offences have had to pass an **extended test** to get their licences back. The courts can also impose a re-test for other endorsable offences.

Since 1997, when the New Drivers Act became law, people who have accumulated six penalty points or more during their first two years of driving have their licence revoked. (This includes points for offences committed before passing the Driving Test.) They have to reapply for a provisional licence, and pass their Theory and Practical tests again.

Note: you may be surprised to learn that recent statistics indicate about 1,000 drivers have to do this every month.

The Extended Test

Drivers ordered to take an extended test also have to reapply for a provisional licence and pass the Theory Test. The extended test is **longer** and **more demanding** than the ordinary driving test, and there is a **higher fee.**

The extended test focuses particularly on the driver's skills of **concentration,** and their **attitude** to other road users, since these are the areas that may well have brought them before the courts.

GETTING THE BALANCE RIGHT

In recent years, schemes have been introduced to provide the option of **re-training** rather than prosecution for drivers who have committed errors that are careless rather than dangerous. The drivers undertake training at their own expense.

The government are looking at ways to expand this initiative, with a view to making re-testing part of a more flexible and positive approach that combines the extended test with effective training.

RE-TESTING FOR OLDER DRIVERS

When drivers reach the age of 70 they have to renew their licence and confirm that they are fit to continue driving. There have been some calls for a formal test at this stage, but it is not clear what this would include or where it would take place.

For example, would the test be confined to the routes which the driver normally uses (see 'Older drivers and self-regulation', page 37) or would they be required to demonstrate their fitness to drive on all kinds of roads, including motorways?

This kind of test could result in anxiety and reluctance to take the test, and might deter some people from continuing to drive – especially if there was an impact on their insurability.

There have also been calls for **eye tests,** especially of **night vision,** because this often deteriorates as people get older (see page 36). But once again, most people adapt their driving to times and places where they know they are safe and will not endanger others.

As more people continue driving into their 80s, it may be that the drivers themselves will become actively involved in deciding how best to ensure safe driving for all.

Surveys show that drivers with the worst night vision have the fewest night-time accidents.

TEST YOUR UNDERSTANDING
OF THIS SECTION

1. Under what circumstances must drivers take an extended test?

2. How does the extended test differ from the normal driving test?

3. What are some of the difficulties involved in setting up a compulsory re-test for older drivers?

Answers on page 207

Answers

Part 1 answers

ANSWERS TO QUESTIONS ON 'WHY PEOPLE CHOOSE TO UNDERTAKE FURTHER TRAINING'

1. People undertake further training for a variety of reasons relating to life experiences or crises, or as a result of an employer's requirement if they have to drive for their work.

    People who have just passed their test may go on to book extra lessons in motorway driving, and to get experience of a wide range of traffic conditions with the help of an instructor.

    Older drivers sometimes experience a lack of confidence, and embark on a course of training to restore it. They may also wish to catch up with developments that have occurred since they passed their driving test.

    Some couples leave all the driving to one partner, so that if that person becomes ill or dies, the other has a need to renew their driving skills as well as receiving reassurance from an expert that they are capable of coping with today's traffic.

2. If you wish to take a test in advanced driving, you may choose to follow a course with the Institute of Advanced Motorists (IAM). They feature a combination of lectures and practical guidance leading to a certificate and badge. There is a members' magazine, and social activities are organised by local groups. Some discounts are offered to drivers with IAM certificates; for example, discounts on insurance or breakdown cover.

    The Royal Society for the Prevention of Accidents have their own Advanced Drivers' Association, and operate tests for cars, LGVs, motorcycles, minibuses and scooters. They award certificates graded Gold, Silver and Bronze.

    In addition to IAM and RoSPA, many private companies have been set up to offer a range of customised courses for company drivers. They guarantee to reduce accidents, enabling companies to reduce running costs, maintenance and insurance premiums.

The AA's Fleet Driver Training courses are taught by Approved Driving Instructors specially selected by the AA for their skills and knowledge. All undergo a further training course themselves before they commence working in FDT.

3. Fleet Driver Training may lead to a test, such as that offered by the IAM, but it does not necessarily do so. The way the training is organised can be flexible to suit the requirements of the company or individual; often the instructor covers a series of skills and tells the person undertaking the training how they would score in each, and how they might improve certain aspects for the future.

In addition, specific techniques are demonstrated which would not be appropriate for learners, but which can benefit drivers with more experience. Instructors will bear in mind

that you have already passed your test, so you are simply seeking to improve on what should already be good driving.

ANSWERS TO QUESTIONS ON 'THE RIGHT ATTITUDE'

1. One reason given for driver aggression is that society in general is becoming more violent, so that 'road rage' can be seen as a sign of the times. The confined environment of the car, and the frequent occasions when it is impossible to make speedy progress, lead to frustration and anger. As a car driver, one has no choice but to take a high degree of interest in the behaviour of others, because their mistakes can put you at risk of injury, or damage to your property. High levels of noise, or weather conditions such as heat and humidity, can encourage aggression in drivers. A final point is that almost all cars on the roads are capable of extremely high performance, but it is almost impossible to take advantage of this most of the time.

2. Defensive driving involves practising hazard awareness skills at all times, and making the assumption that other road users may make errors. Maintain a position on the road which allows you to take evasive action if necessary, and do not drive so fast that you could not stop in an emergency. Ensure you have adequate space for carrying out manoeuvres such as overtaking, and do not engage in aggressive driving that could unnerve and intimidate others.

3. Business drivers are under particular pressures due to arrival time deadlines – sometimes several in the course of a day. The culture of the company may be such that though outwardly applauding safe driving, it may place expectations on employees, which result in stress and aggression. Companies who have invested in qualified driver training are demonstrating a willingness to address these problems.

4. The Government's Road Safety Strategy and casualty reduction targets aim to ensure that our roads become significantly safer for all by the end of the first decade of this century.

    The DETR document acknowledges that there is currently no generally accepted industry standard for qualified driver training, but foresees a wider role for organisations that offer training in developing a safer driving culture.

The DSA, in cooperation with RoSPA, IAM and others, will be working to set a benchmark for accreditation of advanced driving, and to register training organisations and specialist instructors.

The HSE Task Force dealing with work-related journeys will establish accurate accident statistics and look into causes and prevention. They will agree minimum standards for employers in managing the safety of work-related journeys, and set up liaison between those who enforce road traffic law and those who enforce health and safety at work.

ANSWERS TO QUESTIONS ON 'KEEPING UP WITH CHANGE'

1. In order to pass the Theory Test, drivers must have a thorough knowledge of *The Highway Code*. Books and CDs that include the official questions and answers can be helpful in preparation for the test, but it is neither desirable nor possible to learn the questions off by heart, since there are nearly a thousand possible questions at the time of writing, and they are frequently changed. It has been proved that the learning needed to pass the Theory Test has a positive effect in road safety terms for the learner driver.

2. The Theory Test is administered by the Driving Standards Agency (DSA), who set the questions and arrange times and centres for tests. There are 35 questions to answer in 40 minutes, using a touch-screen method. The questions cover a range of topics including: alertness, attitude and hazard awareness; vehicle handling and loading; speed limits and safety margins; legal documents; road and traffic signs; rules of the road; and what to do in an accident. Learners must pass this test before they can apply for their Practical Test; the Practical Test must then be taken, and passed, within two years.

3. Some recent changes to the Practical Test include a lengthening of the time allocated to each test to 55 minutes, to allow time for the inclusion of more varied and faster roads. The set exercises have been amended to provide more flexibility for the examiner, and to give the candidate a chance to demonstrate how well they drive overall. This includes observing and reacting to hazards, and being aware of all signs and signals.

    Reverse parking (into a marked bay, or behind a parked car) has been added to the set exercises; the candidate now has to perform two out of three, the others being reversing round a corner and turning in a road (this exercise was formerly known as 'the three point turn', but may involve more than three movements). The emergency stop may be tested on a random basis.

ANSWERS TO QUESTIONS ON 'YOU NEVER STOP LEARNING'

1. Newly-qualified drivers can benefit from extra lessons covering aspects they did not need to learn for the driving test, and to build confidence on motorways and other fast roads.

2. Hazard awareness skills develop steadily over time as experience is gained on a wide variety of roads and in all kinds of traffic conditions. After passing the test the driver is still concentrating on controlling the car, but when those skills have become automatic there is more time available for scanning the road ahead, and spotting hazards that are building up at the edge of one's field of vision.

3. There is a temptation to exceed the speed limit at the start or end of a restricted zone (for example, on approaching a village), or on a road, which looks 'fast' but which nevertheless, has a lower limit. Newly qualified drivers can feel pressurised by impatient drivers behind, and may inadvertently exceed the limit.

4. Some drivers will show extra consideration when following a vehicle displaying a P-plate; however, it can unfortunately act as a target for some people, causing them to tailgate and harass the probationer driver. The Government's current road safety strategy gives serious consideration to introducing the compulsory use of P-plates, because of the known high accident rates among newly qualified drivers.

5. Planning your route thoroughly in advance will make your journey more successful, as you will avoid wasting time through taking wrong turnings etc. For short journeys, if you know you have to travel at a busy time to a destination which you have not visited before, it can make sense to do a practice run when traffic is light, to prevent stress later. Longer journeys will benefit from a list of points along the route typed out clearly and correctly. Don't forget to plan an alternative route, in case you encounter problems with the one you originally selected.

6. We are seeing many more older drivers on our roads due to increased life expectancy for people generally, and the way in which the car has become a necessary part of most older people's lifestyle. Elderly parents can no longer rely on their children to drive them around, as most will be working; and it has become more usual for women to drive themselves rather than relying on their husbands, as in the past – increased affluence has seen a trend for both partners to own a car. Public transport has become increasingly unreliable, and buses in rural areas have drastically reduced in number, so that many more people today rely on the car.

7. Even though eyesight and mobility may deteriorate in old age, this is compensated for by the accumulated experience of many years behind the wheel; anticipation and hazard awareness improve with age, and older drivers will limit themselves to routes and speeds where they know they feel competent, thus maximising safety. However, there are some aspects of driving where older people experience difficulty, especially manoeuvres that involve reversing or turning right.

8. 'Bad habits' include: crossing hands on the steering wheel; resting the left hand on the gear lever instead of returning it to the wheel; resting an arm on the door through an open window; making excessive use of the gears at the expense of proper use of the brakes; and causing a hazard to following traffic by driving too slowly.

ANSWERS TO QUESTIONS ON 'UNDERSTANDING RISK'

1. Drivers are particularly at risk at road junctions, and places where traffic joins or merges. Reversing manoeuvres can often lead to accidents, as can reckless driving at high speed. Many accidents are also caused by following too closely behind the vehicle in front (tailgating), and by illegal manoeuvres such as 'undertaking' on a three-lane motorway, or hazardously crossing the path of an oncoming vehicle.

2. It is part of being an expert driver to show courtesy to other road users, but such courtesy is misplaced if you wave someone on in a potentially dangerous situation – for example, where visibility is inadequate, or if your action results in following motorists having to brake. At roundabouts there is a clear system of priority – give way to traffic approaching from the right – and you would be causing a hazard if you give way when it is your turn to proceed. (There are of course some exceptions, such as giving way to long vehicles.) It is not safe to wave people on at pedestrian crossings, since another driver might attempt to overtake illegally, or oncoming traffic may not stop.

3. Remember to choose a safe place to reverse, avoiding busy roads and the areas surrounding schools. Look mainly through your rear window, while making use of all mirrors to check for pedestrians and approaching vehicles. Never reverse into a busy road. If you cannot see clearly, try to get someone to help you; get out and look for yourself; or find an alternative way to proceed, such as driving round the block instead of reversing.

4. Many motorists seem to believe: that they are better than the average driver; that speed limits are designed for people with poor reaction times; and that they need not stick strictly to them. Surveys have shown that speeds in a 30mph zone average about 33mph. Keeping to speed limits in residential areas has been proved to save lives. The higher the speed, the higher the chance that an accident victim will be killed rather than injured. But even though drivers may be aware of this, they are likely to

continue exceeding the limit until deterred by fines or even disqualification.

5. There is no reason why you should not choose to drive at a speed slightly under the speed limit for a particular stretch of road, if you are more comfortable doing so or the conditions require it. However, to drive excessively slowly presents a hazard to other road users, especially on a narrow road where visibility is limited, as it will encourage risky overtaking and mounting frustration.

6. Motorways are in fact relatively safe roads to drive on, as traffic is all flowing in one direction and there are long slip roads to enable drivers to build up their speed when joining. The road surface should also be in good condition, though of course there are exceptions. Potential hazards such as learner drivers, cyclists, animals, parked cars, slow vehicles etc are not allowed on the motorway. By contrast there are many more hazards to negotiate in the high street of a busy town, and this is where the highest number of accidents take place.

7. It is safest for small children to travel in the rear seat of your car, preferably in a specially designed integrated child seat. If children are not properly restrained they are at great risk in an accident; they are also a cause of distraction to the driver. *The Highway Code* makes it clear that the safety of child passengers is the driver's responsibility, and gives specific guidance on restraints for children of various ages. Children should never be allowed to ride in the back section of an estate vehicle or hatchback, where there are no seats or seatbelts.

8. If you choose a high-performance car it is likely to encourage you to drive faster, and to take more risks when overtaking. Drivers of cars with a high level of engine noise will tend to drive more slowly, and vice versa. It has been shown that the beneficial effect of including large numbers of safety features in the newest models can be offset by the tendency of drivers to be more careless, because they are relying on the design of their car and not their skills as a driver.

Part 2 answers

ANSWERS TO QUESTIONS ON 'HAZARD PERCEPTION'

1. Hazard perception skills improve progressively with age, and people who have been driving for many years are up to two seconds faster in reacting to hazards than novice drivers (i.e., people who have been driving for three years or less). However, training is very effective in making up for lack of experience, and will result in both improvement in hazard perception, and driving with less risk than before.

2. Commentary driving is favoured by instructors of advanced driving because it enhances concentration and helps you focus more carefully on the road ahead. You can try it out by commenting out loud on all the possible hazards you come across as you drive, and how you will deal with each of them in turn. Your ability to process visual information, and select the most important elements, should also improve.

3. Video films of traffic scenes are shown to drivers, who are asked to press a button when they spot a potential danger facing the car driver. The results are collated and the instructor gives each person an assessment of how well they are doing. The film can then be re-run so that the instructor can point out hazards that were missed. This method seems to have a positive effect on hazard perception, because the images remain in people's memory so that they are more aware the next time they see a similar hazard in real life.

4. Some everyday hazards include: road junctions, roundabouts, traffic lights, slow vehicles, motorcycles, bicycles, pedestrians, parked vehicles, horse-riders, roadworks, buses and trams, school entrances, pedestrian crossings, level crossings, fords, uneven surfaces and adverse weather. There are of course many others which are unusual or 'one-off', including road accidents.

ANSWERS TO QUESTIONS ON 'OBSERVATION'

1. Scanning involves training your eyes to take in all the important information in your range of vision – as opposed to idly looking around without noting the significance of what you see. You should alternately look ahead as far as possible and near – and use your mirrors to complete the picture.

2. You need to make an extra effort to be observant when driving at twilight, or in the glare of a low sun. It can be difficult at such times to judge how far away other vehicles are, and your observation skills can suffer when you are tired. (Don't forget to scan down to middle distance as well as just ahead of you.)

3. Rubbish sacks piled by the roadside indicate that you may shortly have to slow down for a dustcart. Be prepared to overtake safely, or to follow at slow speed if it is not safe to overtake. This is just one of the clues you need to be aware of every day.

4. Road markings give you information about speed limits, parking restrictions and about which lane to select when approaching a roundabout. An inverted triangle on the road warns you of a junction. Zigzag lines are used at the approaches to pedestrian crossings, to indicate that you should not park or overtake. See your *Highway Code* for other examples of road markings. As a rule: the more paint on the road, the more danger.

5. The information you receive visually while driving is supported by what your other senses tell you; you may be able to hear or smell potential hazards before you see them, and you can then prepare to take appropriate action. This is especially true of the sirens on police cars, ambulances and other emergency vehicles.

ANSWERS TO QUESTIONS ON 'ANTICIPATION AND PLANNING'

1. Being proactive is vital for safe driving; experience helps you to anticipate hazards and prepare to take evasive action if necessary. Most drivers tend to be reactive rather than proactive.

2. At bends and other places where you have a restricted view, you should take up a position where you can see as much of the road as possible. An example of this is to keep well over to the left at a right-hand bend. Not only will this improve your view, it will also improve the view other drivers have of you; and this technique guarantees you the maximum information on which to base your decision about how to proceed. Equally, move to your right on a left-hand bend for the same reason – but only as far as you feel comfortable, and not over the centre line.

3. Making successful progress is not linked to travelling at high speeds. Anticipating hazards in advance means you are unlikely to be forced into making decisions; you will be less stressed and drive more safely, and your average speed will

probably be the same as that of someone whose driving style consists of accelerating rapidly and braking suddenly.

4. If the exit you want is 'after 12 o'clock', select the right-hand lane. At some complex roundabouts you may have to use the information on the road surface as a guide.

5. You should begin indicating at the first of the three blue and white countdown markers which are positioned ahead of the slip road.

6. Experienced drivers will pick up clues all the time when driving, processing information received from their eyes and ears, and on occasion using their other senses too. The clues provide invaluable advance warnings of hazards ahead, and you will find that as you acquire more experience, you become more skilled at linking what you observe to what you are likely to encounter next.

7. Normally traffic on a motorway is moving constantly at high speeds and all three (or more) lanes are in use. If you are travelling in the centre or the

outside lane, you should have an 'escape plan' ready to use in the event of a breakdown or accident involving your own vehicle or others, since it may be difficult to move quickly to the inside lane. You should not stay in the outside lane once others become available, and you should avoid being forced to travel in a 'sandwich' in the centre lane. Do not resort to driving along the hard shoulder, unless signs direct you to do so when roadworks and contraflows are in operation.

8. You should keep well back when following long vehicles, as they need extra space to manoevre at roundabouts and junctions, and take longer to slow down than small vehicles when they are travelling at speed. Motorcyclists also need longer to stop, and are less stable than cars, so you should be aware that they may be blown across your path by high winds.

9. Different people have different reaction times, depending on age, health and experience – for example, a racing driver's

reaction times are likely to be much faster than average. Your speed of reaction will have an impact on how fast you can stop in an emergency. The recommended stopping distances given in *The Highway Code* can only represent an average, and it is always best to allow rather more margin for error.

Part 3 answers

ANSWERS TO QUESTIONS ON 'USING THE CONTROLS'

1. The major function of the Driving Test at present is to assess how competent you are at controlling the car safely and smoothly (although other aspects are assessed through the Theory Test). Research has shown that there is no correlation between performance in the Driving Test and subsequent involvement in accidents. This is why the Government places such a high priority on providing training in hazard perception.

2. When the vehicle is accelerating, the weight is transferred from the front wheels to the back. For front-wheel drive cars this means that the driving wheels have less grip, so that there is a risk of wheel-spin in slippery conditions. Rear-wheel drive vehicles, on the other hand, gain more grip on the driving wheels during acceleration. For four-wheel drive vehicles the effects will vary depending on how the power is distributed between the front and back wheels in each individual model – consult the manufacturer's handbook for information.

3. The gears enable you to select the power you need from the engine in order to perform various tasks.

4. When approaching traffic lights, you should use your skills of anticipation and observation to judge whether you are likely to need to stop. Control your speed by using engine braking or applying the foot brake to give a signal to the drivers behind; you should not 'drift' towards the lights, going downwards through the gears, in the hope that you will not have to stop.

5. The vehicle becomes less stable when going round a bend, so it is best to keep both hands on the wheel to maintain maximum control. If it is necessary to change gear, then do not change while turning the steering wheel – wait until the wheel is in a holding position.

6. 'Engine braking' occurs when you ease off the accelerator and the vehicle naturally begins to slow. More controlled braking is achieved by use of the footbrake.

   'Cadence braking' is a technique that is useful in correcting skidding on ice or slippery road surfaces; it involves applying the brake briefly to slow the vehicle, then releasing it in order to steer, then repeating this pattern several times. You only use it if and when the brakes lock up and cause a skid, and **never** use it with ABS.

7. Steering 'hand-over-hand', as opposed to 'feeding the wheel' through your hands in a controlled manner, is a dangerous habit because: if you were to do this on a bend and the curve of the road suddenly increased, you would be left with no opportunity to turn further, and the vehicle could swerve out of control into the path of oncoming traffic.

8. You should not allow the 'centring' mechanism of the wheel to spin it back into position, because while this is taking place you do not have adequate control of the vehicle.

9. The basic method for dealing with a rear-wheel skid is to try to steer first in the direction of the skid until the tyres regain some grip on the road, and then attempt to steer in the desired direction again. But it is preferable to use your anticipation skills to avoid going into a skid, and take care not to indulge in either harsh braking or excessive acceleration, both common causes of skidding.

10. If you switch to driving a vehicle fitted with power-assisted steering, after driving one that does not have it, you will notice a tendency to 'oversteer'. However, you should soon become accustomed to the different feel of the steering.

ANSWERS TO QUESTIONS ON 'USING THE LIGHTS AND MIRRORS'

1. When on main beam the headlights should be directed roughly horizontally; when on dipped, they should be angled downwards correctly by a garage.

2. You should always use dipped headlights in the daytime when visibility is poor – in rain, mist or fog, or on a generally dull day. Your headlights enable you to see and be seen.

3. Foglights should only be used when visibility is seriously reduced. They should never be used to harass or intimidate other road users.

4. Always make sure that your headlights are correctly adjusted, so that you do not dazzle other road users when driving at night. Be aware of other road users when driving on unlit roads, and switch back to dipped headlights when following another vehicle or when traffic is approaching. Do not switch on foglights if you can see more than 100m (330ft),

and switch them off as soon as visibility improves.

5. According to *The Highway Code*, the only reason for flashing your lights at other drivers is to alert them to your presence.

6. While you are following another vehicle you should drive on dipped headlights – never use your main beam to intimidate others. When you move out to overtake, stay on dipped headlights until you draw level with the other vehicle, and then switch to main beam if necessary and appropriate.

7. Hazard warning lights may be used when stationary only to warn other traffic if your vehicle has broken down and is causing an obstruction. You may switch on your hazard warning lights for a short time while driving on some motorways if you need to alert other road users to a hazard ahead.

8. When changing lanes frequent use of the mirrors is vital for safety. This applies to pulling out into another lane on an urban

road just as much as to changing lanes at high speed on a motorway or dual carriageway. Always use your mirrors in plenty of time to ensure you will not cause following traffic to swerve or stop abruptly.

9. You can find out the extent of your 'blind spot' by noting when a vehicle that is overtaking you on a motorway disappears from view. A quick glance over your shoulder to compensate for the blind spot is acceptable, but it would be dangerous to turn completely round in your seat, as you could collide with the vehicle ahead.

10. Looking in your left mirror can help you judge how far you are from the kerb or edge of the road, or from a vehicle on your left, and to check no one is trying to drive up on your left-hand side when exiting a roundabout.

ANSWERS TO QUESTIONS ON 'HINTS ON PARKING AND OVERTAKING'

1. Try to choose a space that is at least one-and-a-half times the length of your car.

2. Position your vehicle parallel with the vehicle in front of the space, and about two or three feet away from it. Your bonnet should be in line with its bumper.

3. Turn the steering wheel to the left first, until the offside rear corner of your car is aligned with the nearside front corner of the car behind. Next, turn the wheel to the right and continue to reverse, finishing with your wheels parallel to the kerb.

4. Places where you are not allowed to park include: on a motorway (including the hard shoulder); on a Clearway; in bus, cycle or tram lanes during their hours of operation; on the approach to a pedestrian crossing (or on the crossing itself); on the approach to a level crossing; in a space reserved for Blue Card holders; obstructing entrances and exits; at a bus stop; opposite or within 10 metres (32 feet) of a junction;

and all roads indicated by white, yellow or red line markings and qualified by times, etc, on a sign near by.

5.   Before overtaking you should ask yourself, 'Is it safe? Is it legal? Is it necessary?'

6.   Your local knowledge will provide you with clues about whether you need to overtake, or whether the obstruction will shortly disappear, removing the need for overtaking. For example, there may be a dual carriageway just ahead.

7.   Never overtake when approaching a junction; or on the brow of a hill, on a bend, or when approaching a humpback bridge. Do not overtake unless you are sure you have sufficient space to carry out the manoeuvre without inconveniencing or endangering other road users. Do not overtake if it means crossing double white lines – unless you need to overtake a stationary vehicle, or one travelling at 10mph or less. Observe all road signs for 'No Overtaking'.

8.   You should be especially careful when overtaking a long vehicle because it can be difficult to see far enough ahead of them. You can deal with this by dropping back further to increase your field of vision, and to check whether there is another long vehicle ahead of the one you're planning to overtake. Make sure you have enough room to complete the entire manoeuvre in safety.

ANSWERS TO QUESTIONS ON 'DEALING WITH ROUNDABOUTS AND JUNCTIONS'

1. Any place where traffic joins or merges is hazardous for drivers, and roundabouts and junctions demand care and concentration. T-junctions and staggered junctions are frequently the locations for accidents.

2. When turning into a side road look out for cyclists just behind you, and for pedestrians crossing the side road – they have priority if they have already started to cross.

3. Advanced stop lines are provided at some junctions to enable cyclists and/or buses to position themselves ahead of other traffic. Motorists must wait behind these lines, and allow time for the cyclists or buses to move off when the lights change.

4. As you approach the roundabout look ahead and to the right to assess the speed and volume of traffic on the roundabout; indicate if appropriate, and move smoothly into the flow. Do not proceed at speed while still looking to the right, or you will run the risk of colliding with traffic ahead of you. Remember that some complex roundabouts involve priority to vehicles on a major route through the roundabout.

5. A cluster of mini-roundabouts can be confusing if you are not familiar with the area, and a 'satellite cluster' (or magic roundabout) can appear a nightmare. Don't panic. You should treat each as a separate roundabout and apply the rules to each in turn. When on a magic roundabout, they are surprisingly easy to deal with, and very efficient at moving traffic. Be on the lookout, however, for other motorists who may be confused and not giving clear signals.

6. If you are not sure which exit you will need to take at a roundabout it is advisable to select the right-hand lane so that you can review the options in turn, rather than being forced to leave the roundabout sooner than you intend. Use clear signals and do not cut across traffic in other lanes. If possible, have your route fully planned in advance, but this may not always be possible where roundabouts are concerned, especially where new ones have been introduced.

ANSWERS TO QUESTIONS ON 'SIGNALLING AND LANE DISCIPLINE'

1. Indicator signals provide advance warning and information about your movements to other road users – cyclists, pedestrians etc as well as car drivers. You should give a clear signal in plenty of time before moving out from a stationary position, slowing down, turning left or right, changing lanes, leaving roundabouts, and overtaking. Always check your mirrors before you signal, and then carry out the manoeuvre if it is safe to do so.

2. Signals are only necessary if there is other traffic around, or other road-users who need to know what you are doing. Thus, it would not be necessary to signal when driving along an empty road, or when moving off if there are no vehicles in the vicinity. Some learners are taught to signal whenever they pass a parked vehicle, but this would be excessive if driving along a road lined with parked cars.

3. You should sound your horn only to let other road users know you are there – never as an audible signal of annoyance. You must not sound your horn: when the vehicle is stationary (except when you believe yourself to be in danger from another person or vehicle); or at animals; or when driving in a built-up area between 11.30pm and 7am (except in an emergency).

4. If you can select the correct lane at traffic lights you will avoid holding up others or being held up yourself, and will be able to make the most effective progress. Try to look ahead of the lights and note whether any lanes are about to merge; this will assist your choice.

5. You must not drive in any lane reserved for buses or trams within its hours of operation, or in cycle lanes. When driving on motorways, be on the lookout for advance warning of lanes that are closed, and resist the temptation to speed ahead and then force your way into the available lane at the last minute.

ANSWERS TO QUESTIONS ON 'DRIVING FOR ECONOMY'

1. If most of your driving is done in town, driving in low gears with frequent stops and starts, a car with a small engine is likely to be your best choice for fuel economy. However, don't forget that the most economical (and healthiest!) choice of all is to leave the car at home for short journeys, and walk or cycle instead.

2. Keeping your car windows closed will keep turbulence to a minimum and reduce drag, so improving fuel economy.

3. You cannot entirely avoid using more fuel when you are driving on busy urban roads with frequent hazards and obstructions (such as parked or turning vehicles, roadworks etc). But you can use your skills of anticipation and forward planning to maintain the most smooth progress possible in the conditions, and use space management to ensure you are not constantly having to brake sharply when a vehicle stops ahead.

4. 'Coasting' the vehicle means driving downhill with the clutch down or with the gears in 'neutral', as a means of saving fuel. This is an unsafe technique as you do not have sufficient control of the vehicle; on a steep gradient it could easily run away with you, as engine braking is not operating; and you will lose all power assistance to the steering and brakes if the engine should stall.

Part 4 answers

ANSWERS TO QUESTIONS ON 'OBSERVING SPEED LIMITS'

1. An 'inappropriate speed' is one which is higher than is safe for the road and traffic conditions, and which is likely to lead to loss of control and thus to accidents. There are many occasions when it is not possible to drive at the highest speed allowed for the road you are on – either because of density of traffic, or because weather conditions demand a lower speed.

2. Speed limits have been shown to reduce accidents, because whenever a new speed limit is introduced or an existing one is changed, drivers will take note and adjust their speed, since they do not want to risk being caught speeding. Where 30mph limits are enforced in and around residential areas, fewer pedestrians will be injured or killed – and if someone is hit by a moving vehicle, their chances of survival are greater when the vehicle is travelling at a relatively low speed. (They may survive at 20mph, but at 40mph they will usually die.)

3. The speed limits listed in *The Highway Code* for different types of roads are: 30mph in built-up areas, 60mph on other single-carriageway roads, and 70mph for motorways and dual carriageways. These limits apply only when no other speed limit is indicated by road signs and markings. For larger and heavier vehicles, and those towing trailers, lower limits apply; look these up in your *Highway Code.*

4. Speed limits are a cause of frustration to the average law-abiding motorist, especially when they receive points on their licence for a one-off offence, perhaps committed when they allowed their attention to wander briefly. Giving more flexibility to the courts could provide an opportunity to impose tougher penalties for more serious offences, and could target dangerous drivers and regular offenders.

ANSWERS TO QUESTIONS ON 'MANAGING DISTRACTIONS'

1. Experienced drivers rely on automatic responses for many regular actions and manoeuvres, including gear changing and pedal control. An automatic sequence may also develop on journeys carried out on a regular basis, so that you always select the same gear to negotiate a particular roundabout, or the same lane at a junction. The danger here is that you may fail to notice, for example, a change in road layout, or fail to slow down in time before an unexpected hazard. Familiarity breeds contempt.

2. Holding a conversation with a passenger, or on a mobile phone, has been shown to reduce hazard awareness in experienced drivers to a level little better than that of newly-qualified drivers. You have to be firm with yourself and with others about the absolute necessity of concentration in difficult traffic conditions.

3. At one time it was thought that using a hands-free mobile phone was quite safe, because you were able to remain in control of the gears, steering etc while talking on the phone. However, it has been proved that this is not the case – your mind is focused on the phone call and not on controlling the car. The best advice is to stop in a safe place to make or respond to telephone calls.

4. 'Rubber-necking' is the name given to the actions of drivers craning their necks to see what has happened at the scene of an accident. As well as being a deplorable habit it is also highly dangerous, since the drivers concerned are being distracted from the road ahead; and the resultant slowing down of traffic leads to the swift formation of queues and delays.

ANSWERS TO QUESTIONS ON 'AVOIDING ACCIDENTS'

1. Tailgating is a dangerous habit often associated with driver aggression. If you are following another vehicle too closely you risk having a collision if the driver in front is forced to stop suddenly. You should also leave sufficient room to manoeuvre if the vehicle in front breaks down. Following a long vehicle too closely is especially risky because you cannot see clearly ahead to overtake. You should resist the temptation to tailgate in fog.

2. You should increase your separation distance in adverse weather, to at least four seconds in rain and twenty seconds in icy conditions. This is necessary because the grip of your tyres is diminished. Any other hazards such as flooding or mud on the road should also alert you to increase the gap.

3. You should overtake only when you can see clearly that there is sufficient space for you to do so safely and without endangering any other road user, or causing traffic on the opposite carriageway to slow down.

4. Do not overtake on a bend, on the brow of a hill, or near a junction, or in any place where road signs and lines on the road indicate that overtaking is forbidden. Do not overtake where cross-hatched areas separate the two streams of traffic. When overtaking stationary vehicles on your side of the road, give way to traffic from the opposite direction.

5. It is sometimes advantageous to drop down a gear, for example when overtaking a slow-moving vehicle on a hill; this will increase engine speed and supply the necessary acceleration to enable you to carry out the manoeuvre promptly and in safety.

6. Before overtaking you should always ask yourself: Is it safe? Is it legal? Is it necessary?

ANSWERS TO QUESTIONS ON 'DRIVING AT NIGHT AND DEALING WITH TIREDNESS'

1. At night there is usually less traffic on the road, and there may be fewer hazards to negotiate; for example, roadworks are often suspended overnight. The lights of oncoming vehicles can warn you of their presence before the vehicle itself comes into view.

2. Even if the roads are clearer than in the day, you should be prepared to drive more slowly, because your field of vision is more limited and it can be difficult to judge distances. If you are dazzled by another vehicle's headlights, your first response should be to slow down; your eyes will need time to readjust after the glare has receded.

3. Pedestrians and cyclists are most at risk at night, since motorists may not see them unless they are wearing light-coloured clothing or reflective armbands etc. Children walking home from school in the winter months are especially vulnerable, because their ability to judge distances is not fully developed and they are often not aware that there is traffic approaching.

4. Business drivers are known to be at risk of falling asleep on daytime journeys, especially on long uninterrupted stretches of motorway where there is little to stimulate alertness, and on routine journeys where there is a temptation to drive 'on autopilot'.

5. 'DWA' stands for 'driving without awareness', a term used by police to describe the circumstances in (4).

6. Plan your route in advance and build in time for one or more breaks. Eat regular light snacks and drink sufficient non-alcoholic fluids to keep you alert; 'sports' or 'energy' drinks are a good alternative to coffee. Take a short walk, and on a very long journey build in time for a short nap. Listen to music or travel news if you find this helpful. Avoid travelling at times when you know you will be prone to sleepiness.

7. Two hours is probably the longest stretch you could safely drive without a break. You should also consider the comfort of your passengers.

8. If you drive in an aggressive manner and engage in mental conflict with other drivers, this will produce stress and use up energy which should be directed towards your driving. Practise putting aside other problems during driving time so that you can concentrate on the task in hand.

9. You are at the greatest risk of falling asleep at the wheel between midnight and 6am, but the urge to sleep can be just as strong between 2-4pm in the afternoon.

10. Going for a walk and opening the car window can assist in restoring awareness, but research suggests that the most reliable method is to find a safe place to stop for a short nap, and drink one or more cans of a 'sports' or 'energy' drink.

ANSWERS TO QUESTIONS ON 'DRIVING A NEW OR UNFAMILIAR VEHICLE'

1. You should familiarise yourself with the gear lever positions for all gears, remembering that the technique for selecting reverse can vary in different vehicles. Find out how to operate the lights and windscreen wipers, and make sure your seat is correctly adjusted so that you can reach the pedals comfortably.

2. Reading through the manual will help you to find out about the vehicle's controls and instrument panel, and give you information about warning lights. The location of the switches may be different from that in vehicles you have previously driven, so take time to check all of these, as well as how to access the fuel tank, open the bonnet, etc.

3. In an automatic car you will usually find 'park', 'reverse', 'neutral' and three forward. The vehicle should be left in park when you leave the car, but use neutral when stationary in traffic; and you must select 'drive' for the vehicle to move forwards. You should place your

right foot on the brake and lift it slowly, moving the same foot to the accelerator as you pick up speed. The automatic transmission will change the gears up and down, although you must select reverse manually, and you may wish to select a lower gear to gain acceleration, for example when overtaking on a hill.

ANSWERS TO QUESTIONS ON 'DRIVING ABROAD'

1. When driving on the right for the first time you could experience problems with space management; for example, moving out sufficiently far when overtaking parked vehicles. If you are driving a right-hand-drive vehicle you need to pull out earlier to see clearly ahead for any overtaking manoeuvre. You also have to take care when negotiating roundabouts in an unfamiliar direction.

2. You should do as much research as you can in advance about the motoring laws and traffic signs of the country you plan to visit. Find out about road tolls and how they are paid, and plan routes in advance as far as possible, remembering that you should not attempt to drive too far in one stretch until you are used to the conditions and the way local people drive.

3. Do not expect speed limits to be signed in the same way as in the UK. You should take careful note of the speed limit notification in case there are no subsequent reminders along the way. Drivers

breaking the speed limit can incur a heavy on-the-spot fine.

4. Tolls are often in operation on motorway-style roads; you may have to pay at the start or the end of the toll-road, depending on where you are travelling from. Traffic police on motorway-style roads in some countries are able to monitor your speed between toll-booths and impose fines where necessary.

5. You should have with you the passports and visas for yourself and your passengers, your UK driving licence (supplemented by an IDP if appropriate), travel and vehicle insurance documents, and your original Vehicle Registration Document. Keep these in a safe place, readily available for inspection.

6. An International Driving Licence (IDP) is available for a small fee from selected main post offices. You will need to provide a passport-sized photograph signed on the back, and copies of your UK driving licence and identifying passport pages. Note that the IDP is not a 'stand-alone' document, and must be carried along with your UK licence while you are abroad. In some countries it is recommended you carry an IDP, and in others the police will expect to see photographic evidence of identity if you do not have a 'photocard' licence; check with the AA for UK driving information.

7. Useful equipment to carry in your vehicle includes spare keys and light bulbs, spare tyre, tool kit and jack, First Aid kit and red warning triangle. Some of these items are compulsory in some countries, ie, you are required by law to carry them in your vehicle. If you are travelling to a country where you might encounter deep snow and ice, carry snow chains, spade and rope; for hot climates, always take a large container of drinking water in case you become stranded, and invest in an electronic device that will identify your location if you break down in a remote place.

8. Many travel guides, such as those published by the AA, will include a section on allowances. You can also check on the HM Customs

and Excise website at www.hmce.gov.uk. If you are concerned about any matter regarding the illegal importation of tobacco and alcohol, you can call the HM Customs and Excise freephone number at any time – 0800 59 5000. All calls are confidential.

ANSWERS TO QUESTIONS ON 'LOADING YOUR VEHICLE'

1. You are most likely to notice an adverse effect on your vehicle's handling when you make a change of direction, or when you negotiate a sharp or unexpected bend.

2. It is the legal responsibility of the driver of the vehicle to check that it is not overloaded.

3. You can find out what size of load you are qualified to tow from the information printed on your driving licence. For example, a driver may be licensed to drive vehicles in groups A and E with a maximum laden weight (including trailer) of not more than 3.5 tonnes.

4. Passengers are not allowed to travel in a caravan while it is being towed. It would be impossible for them to be safely strapped in, and they would be in a very hazardous situation in the event of an accident or the trailer becoming uncoupled at speed.

ANSWERS TO QUESTIONS ON 'MECHANICAL KNOW-HOW'

1. You should stop immediately if the red oil warning light comes on; to continue driving could seriously damage the engine.

2. You should check the oil level before you start the vehicle, and preferably after it has been stationary for some time. The vehicle should be parked on a level surface if you are to get an accurate reading.

3. *The Highway Code* stipulates a tread depth of at least 1.6mm 'across the central three-quarters of the breadth of the tread and in a continuous band around the entire circumference'. However, 2mm is perhaps a better guide. The figure of 1.6mm applies to cars, light vans and light trailers; for motorcycles, larger vehicles and those that carry passengers, it is 1mm.

4. To check that your rear lights are working, ask someone to help you by standing in a position where they can see the rear of your vehicle. If this is not possible, you may be able to use a reflective surface, such as a garage door, to check that they are working.

5. Checks to be made by your garage include: filters, fluids and brakes; plus battery, distributor cap, clutch cable, spark plugs, HT leads and engine management systems.

6. You are allowed to switch on your hazard warning lights in the event of a breakdown, as a warning to other road users that your vehicle is causing an obstruction. You should never use them as an excuse for illegal parking, and never while driving – unless you are on a motorway or unrestricted dual carriageway, when you may switch them on for a brief period if you need to warn following drivers of a hazard ahead.

ANSWERS TO QUESTIONS ON 'ROUTE PLANNING'

1. When going on a long or unfamiliar journey, set aside time to plan your route in advance. Remember that there could be road and junction closures, so you will need an alternative route in mind. Write down a list of major towns and junctions, highlighting any potentially confusing manoeuvres; the list can be recorded on a tape to play while you are driving. As a precaution, leave a copy of the route with someone else, especially when you are travelling in remote areas or hazardous weather conditions.

2. When selecting which road atlas to buy, check in the front of the atlas to see whether it is an up-to-date edition – out-of-date mapping will be more of a hindrance than a help. Decide whether a large or smaller scale, or a spiral-bound version, will be of most use to you. Become familiar with the colours used for the different types of road, and also the symbols used on the maps. If you are not sure about how the system of grid references works, find out about this too.

3. In-car telematics can relay information to the business driver to make their journey as trouble-free as possible, by providing dynamic route guidance with warnings of delays ahead and suggestions for diversions. Other services are available, such as information on hotel accommodation, warnings of mechanical faults developing, and identification of the vehicle's location in the event of theft. For fleet managers, vehicle tracking systems make it possible to monitor the movements of their workforce and ensure their time is being used effectively.

4. As with mobile phones, the danger of using an interactive voice-operated system is that the driver's mind is occupied elsewhere, and insufficient attention is being directed to driving.

ANSWERS TO QUESTIONS ON 'ROAD SIGNS'

1. Road narrows on both sides

2. Trams crossing ahead

3. No overtaking

4. Route for pedal cycles only

5. Lane shift on a motorway

6. Separated track and path for cycles and pedestrians

ANSWERS TO QUESTIONS ON 'ACCIDENTS AND FIRST AID'

1. There is a danger of fire from any fuel that has been spilled in the area.

2. You should not offer an injured person anything to drink in case they subsequently need an operation involving a general anaesthetic.

3. If someone is injured and is not breathing, carry out the following procedure: lay the casualty on their back, lift the chin and tilt their head backwards, pinch the nostrils and blow into the mouth until the chest rises. Repeat this every four seconds until the person can breathe unaided.

4. You can be more helpful at the scene of an accident if you have First Aid training. Contact the St John Ambulance or St Andrew's Ambulance Association, or the British Red Cross.

5. If you are involved in an accident, you should stop your vehicle immediately. Make sure you have parked in a safe place.

6. When you have been in an accident, a police officer or

anyone 'with reasonable grounds for requiring them' may ask you for your details. This could include the owners of other vehicles involved in the accident.

7. If no police officers are present at the scene, you must report the accident to the police as soon as possible and in any case within 24 hours.

8. It is possible that the shock of being in an accident will cause you to forget the exact sequence of events and the positions of the vehicles involved, if you do not write it down at the time. A written record can also contain names, addresses and registration numbers of other drivers involved and any witnesses, and a diagram may be useful to refer to when trying to establish the reasons for the accident.

ANSWERS TO QUESTIONS ON 'SECURITY AND YOUR VEHICLE'

1. Put personal possessions out of sight, perhaps locked in the boot. When you leave the vehicle even for a short time, check that windows are closed and lock the doors.

2. You should be quite sure that anyone you lend your vehicle to will take as much care of it as you would yourself. They must be covered by insurance. You must also know them well enough to be sure the vehicle will not be used for illegal purposes.

3. Give some thought to where you will park your vehicle and try not to leave it in lonely or unlit areas. Multi-storey car parks can be a focus for crime if they are not regularly patrolled, but if the car park is usually full day and night and there is plenty of activity, you will find it a safer choice than an empty side street.

4. A person intent on committing a crime will usually select the easiest target, so a vehicle with its owner's details etched indelibly on it is more likely to be passed over in favour of one less easily identified.

ANSWERS TO QUESTIONS ON 'A POSTCRIPT ON RE-TESTING'

1. A re-test is ordered by the courts when a person has been convicted of a serious offence such as dangerous driving. Anyone who has been disqualified from driving has to re-apply for a provisional licence and take the Theory Test again, as well as the extended test.

2. The extended test is by definition longer than the normal driving test and can cover more demanding routes. Drivers are likely to need some formal tuition to pass it. Emphasis is placed on the driver's skills of concentration and their attitude to other road users. The fee for the extended test is higher than for the normal driving test.

3. Any plan to introduce a test to establish whether older people were still competent to drive would be likely to be met with resistance, both on grounds of ageism and because the drivers would feel anxious about scoring test results that might be used to identify them as an insurance risk. Rather than face taking a test, some people may give up driving, with inevitable implications for their lifestyle and mobility. For an assessment scheme to work, it would probably need to be done on a voluntary basis and with reference to the kind of routes which the person habitually uses.

Index

ABS 82
anticipation 63–73, 185–6
automatic cars 81, 135, 136, 199–200

breakdowns 118, 136, 151–2

DIAmond 17
driving test (extended) 171, 207
driving test (practical) 28–9,
    178, 187
driving test (theory) 29–30, 178, 207

First Aid 163–5, 205
four-wheel-drive 20, 136, 187

GEM 17
green issues 110–12, 194

hazards 55–7, 183
health and safety 25, 176–7

IAM 16–17, 174, 175, 177
in-car navigation 120, 156–8, 204

junctions 41–2, 93, 100–3, 181, 192

maintenance 148–51, 203
map reading 154, 155–6, 204
motorway driving 47, 67, 71–2, 93,
    108, 125, 162, 182, 185–6, 190

new drivers 32–4, 54, 57, 119, 170,
    174, 179

observation 59–61, 184
older drivers 36–9, 57, 170–71, 174,
    180, 207

parking 95–6, 190–1
passengers 14, 49–51, 117–8, 145,
    146, 182, 196, 202
planning 63–73, 185–6
police training 18
P-plates 34, 179

rally driving 20
re-testing 170–71, 207
rev-counter 80
reversing 44, 181
road signs 66, 67 8, 114, 139,
    160–2, 205
RoSPA 17, 174, 177
roundabouts 68, 93, 100–103,
    192, 200

safety design 49–51, 146
speeding 22–3, 45–6, 114–5, 179,
    181, 195
stopping distances 72–3, 123

track days 19
two-second rule 123

Womens Motoring Service 18, 20